Called to Heal

CALLED TO HEAL

Susan Schuster Campbell

This book is a reference work, not intended to diagnose, prescribe or treat. The information contained herein is in no way to be considered as a substitute for consultation with a licensed health care professional. It is designed to provide information on traditional uses of herbs and historical folklore remedies.

Published by Lotus Press
P.O. Box 325, Twin Lakes, WI 53181 USA
e-mail: lotuspress@lotuspress.com
web site: www.lotuspress.com
phone: (800)824-6396
First US edition, 2000

Editor: Frances Perryer
Designer: Patricia Moloney
Cover design: Kerry Jobusch

Printed in USA

ISBN: 0-914955-91-8
Library of Congress Control Number: 99-85904

Dedication

A Swazi healer, Mrs Dube, once told me: 'Susan, this is the ancestors' book, the ancestors' project. There is a relationship between your ancestors and ours. This is a powerful combination and contributes to your joy in this work, in your visits, in your contact with the healers. It is the right thing to be doing.'

I dedicate this book to the ancestors and thank them for opening this door to me.

Acknowledgements

My profound gratitude and heartfelt thanks to the traditional healers who so kindly welcomed me into their lives, allowing me to observe and draw my own conclusions; to the dedicated doctors and health professionals who so warmly shared their experiences with me; to my friends and bush photographers, Albert Cohn and Jill Lapato, for staying with me on bumpy roads and long site visits in those early days; to Kevin Campbell for beautiful photography during his and Debra's African adventure; to all the readers in the USA, Africa and Europe who reviewed my many drafts; to Nicholas Combrinck, Publishing Manager of Zebra Press, who believed in this project from the start, and Kate Rogan, my editor, who so graciously kept me on course.

I owe a special thanks to my husband and son, for sharing a spirit of adventure and bringing such delight to this project, and to our lives. Finally, I must thank my mother, Jeanette Kuptz Schuster, who instilled in me a wanderlust without which I never would have left home!

Contents

Preface

On 6 July 1996 my family and I accepted an invitation to visit with traditional healer Nomsa Dlamini in the Orlando East district of Soweto. Though we had lived in southern Africa before, and visited South Africa frequently since 1980, we had never been to Soweto. We were impressed with the tidy houses and friendly neighbours in Nomsa's area. Her peaceful traditional clinic, despite its modern concrete shell, was an evocation of rural Africa. I was surprised that my ten-year-old son seemed uncomfortable. Joseph had tagged along on several site visits as I carried out research on African healers, and had grown relaxed and spontaneous in their presence. This uneasiness concerned me and I decided to keep our visit short.

We sat on woven straw mats while Nomsa 'threw the bones' to divine the ancestors' greetings to us. Though she knew little of our background, Nomsa accurately told of our international life and our recent move from an assignment in Warsaw, Poland. She said we were well protected by strong ancestors who looked after us daily. Throwing the bones again, her mood changed. She looked at me, then at Joseph, and said, 'Your son is having trouble with his heart. A valve on the left side of the heart is not closing properly. This is causing your son to have a sharp pain now and then. The pain worries him.' Joseph had never shown signs of such distress. Perhaps Nomsa was 'receiving' information meant for someone else, not my family? 'No,' Nomsa was adamant, 'the ancestors say this is true for your son.'

Joseph was visibly upset and huddled closer to my husband and me. Unsettled to see him frightened, we swiftly said our farewells. As we left the clinic, I took Nomsa aside. I knew she had been a nursing sister for fifteen years before answering a spiritual call to traditional healing. I expected this medical background to come into play now. 'Take your son to a specialist,' she said. 'Have pictures of his heart taken, soon. The matter can be resolved quickly.' Later that day I quietly rang friends and medical colleagues for a referral to a paediatric cardiologist in Johannesburg, just in case there was something to this.

Despite our weekend efforts to lighten the mood, Joseph remained distressed. Finally he told us a heartbreaking story. For nearly two years, he had been experiencing short, sharp spasms in his heart area, as often as twice a day. Imagining open heart surgery or imminent death, he had been reluctant to speak about his discomfort. For years doctors had told us of our son's high tolerance for pain, but suffering daily heart spasms in silence for two years – this was devastating news.

Early the next week, we sat in the Sandton office of a respected South African paediatric cardiologist. Dr Selwyn Milner put Joseph at ease in minutes. He interviewed us and examined Joseph, with my husband and me at his side, gave him an ECG, then led us all downstairs to do an ultrasound. Surrounded by expensive high-tech equipment, Dr Milner showed us an image of a valve in the left ventricle of Joseph's heart. There was an extra floppy bit of tissue which, when it snaps shut, causes an occasional short, sharp pain.

Joseph's heart condition, mitral valve prolapsed syndrome or 'Barlow Syndrome' – experienced by as many as twenty per cent of the world's population – is named after the South African heart specialist who identified the condition. Apparently our ancestors were looking after us that day, as Dr Milner had worked with Dr Barlow and extensive research on the syndrome was available in Johannesburg, our new home. After the visit to Nomsa and Dr Milner, Joseph's anxiety levels dropped dramatically, as did the frequency of the pain. A physically active child, he is able to manage the condition without medication. The prognosis is good that he will continue to do so for the rest of his life. We are grateful to both the African healer and the European doctor for their help and diagnosis.

Like Nomsa Dlamini, a new breed of gifted, well-educated southern African healer is emerging to bridge the gap between the traditional and modern worlds. During site visits and interviews with over one hundred Xhosa, Zulu, Swazi and Tswana healers, and as many medical professionals, I heard constant testimony to the important link these traditionalists provide in the primary health care chain. Amazing stories were told of selfless healers taking in the infirm, unexpected cures for mental illness, broken bones healing overnight, paralysed patients walking, forewarning and counselling of future events that actually came to pass.

I know I am lucky to have visited the healers' extraordinary lives. I hope you enjoy their stories as much as I have. May they challenge your stereotypes as they did mine and inspire you to allow unexpected gifts into your own lives.

Introduction

southern Africa is blessed with a variety of healers – the traditional birth attendant, the herbalist, the faith healer or prophet and others. I had numerous opportunities to meet all of them, but my focus was on the master healer, the 'possessed' healer, chosen by the ancestors to receive a spiritual calling. (They are also called sangoma or inyanga: I use the two words interchangeably, as did the group of healers with whom I spent time.) 'Possessed', as used by the healers, has a positive connotation and represents a close link with their God through the ancestors.

The herbalist's knowledge is based on years of experience assisting a sangoma or an experienced herbalist. These 'technicians' are able to diagnose in many instances, recommend and treat with herbal remedies, but lack the psychic or spiritual ability that fires the possessed healers. Herbalists are important contributors to the primary health care system and often support the work of the healers mentioned in this book.

Finally, at the opposite end of the spectrum from the true healer – and colouring many people's perceptions of traditional healing by their notoriety – are the witchdoctors. These purveyors of questionable mutis and charms cause enormous harm. They frequently operate at night and focus on retribution. The witchdoctors believe there is an external source, usually another person, responsible for a patient's illness. In contrast, the healers believe each person is responsible for their own healing. Harming another person will never, ever help cure a patient.

True respect for the important work of the traditional healer, the main provider of health care in Africa for centuries, has waned in modern times, partly because of misconceptions about their practice. Today, with a new openness in South Africa and an increasing worldwide curiosity about natural medicine and therapies, the traditional healers are coming into their own and setting the record straight.

'We are not practising witchcraft or promoting evil or harm,' says Nomsa Dlamini, professional nurse and sangoma. 'Traditional healers use only natural substances. We have a deep knowledge of the medicinal properties of our indigenous plants. We are constantly learning, as there are more than five hundred varieties of medicinal plants available to us in southern Africa.'

As studies prove, the benefits of natural remedies, herbs and holistic therapies once considered unscientific have rapidly entered the mainstream of my own country. A growing number of American physicians are now recommending holistic complementary treatments as well as conventional medical therapies. Many medical schools throughout the USA are offering 'integrative medicine' programmes in which the new physicians learn western and alternative treatment.

African traditional healers diagnose illnesses, prescribe and prepare herbal medicines, provide counselling and offer spiritual support as well. Still, many people remain puzzled by the sangomas and confuse their work with that of the witchdoctor. The World Health Organisation defines traditional medicine as '...comprising therapeutic practises that have been in existence, often for hundreds of years, before the development and spread of modern scientific medicine and are still in practise today. These practises vary widely, in keeping with the social and cultural heritage of different countries.' In the social and cultural heritage of southern Africa, witchcraft has existed side by side with traditional healing throughout time.

Witchcraft, with its ritual killings and disturbing black magic, is embedded in African culture. This is just one side of the coin though. On the opposite side is the equally powerful and positive contribution of traditional healing's preventative and curative natural health programme. This creates a dilemma for governments who are challenged to ensure that traditional healers practise in a safe and competent way. Until statutory councils exist to register all traditional healers (including witchdoctors posing as healers), enforcing standards and a code of ethics, patients must accept co-responsibility for their health care. They must be aware and able to discriminate between the legitimate and the harmful.

This may seem a tall order – but some basics of the same process used to choose a reputable western medical doctor can be applied. Ask respected family, friends and colleagues for referrals. What has their personal experience been with the particular traditional healer they recommend? How long has the healer been practising? Where did the healer train? What is his or her speciality? Is she good with children and adults? Is he in contact with local clinics or hospitals should a referral to the medical side be necessary? Does she belong to any professional traditional healer organisation and/or have a network of traditional healers to consult with and refer to? If the answers to these queries are satisfactory, an initial appointment might be scheduled with the healer.

On visiting the healer, notice whether the traditional clinic area is hygienic and tidy. Are the herbal medicines stored in clean containers? Does the traditional healer have a professional and respectful manner? Do you feel comfortable and confident in his or her presence? Is your consultation handled in a private and confidential way? If the answer to any of these questions is no, leave politely but promptly and find another traditional practitioner. There are many gifted and experienced traditional healers to choose from.

Throughout southern Africa's history, there have been various efforts to discredit the African healing tradition. At independence, Mozambique had a colonial penal code which outlawed traditional healing practices and made no attempt to differentiate between sorcery and healing. In Swaziland, remaining legislation from their colonial rule continues to mark traditional healing as illegal. In South Africa, the 1974 Health Act and its 1982 amendment restrict traditional healers' performance of any act related to medical practice. KwaZulu-Natal is the only South African province to recognise traditional healers through the 1891 Natal Code of Bantu Law and the KwaZulu Act of 1981. In spite of prohibitive laws, traditional health care has survived and continues to operate as a well-established system in both urban and rural areas, serving a large clientele crossing all educational and socio-economic levels.

In practice, traditional healers are not generally bothered by the legal authorities. On certain issues, such as those surrounding HIV and Aids, cooperative relationships are steadily growing between modern medical and traditional health care practitioners. Institutional changes are also taking place as major businesses recognise traditional healers as important to their employees' health. Since 1994, the South African electric utility, Eskom, has allowed employees to claim a number of visits to traditional healers on the company's medical plan. The South African Medical and Burial Savings Scheme has screened and recognised more than forty traditional healers whom clients are free to consult. The Chamber of Mines and the National Union of Mineworkers of South Africa now allow a panel of traditional healers at the mines and grant their employees three days of leave to consult any healer on the panel. The 105 000-member strong South African Commercial Catering and Allied Workers Union is negotiating a similar policy. In 1966, the Thamba medical aid scheme was formed by the South African Council of Traditional Healers. As of January 1977, Thamba had registered 6 000 healers who offer health services to an estimated three million people.

The medical schools at the universities of Pretoria, Witwatersrand and Cape Town all include discussions of and site visits to traditional clinics in their current community or public health programmes. The psychology departments of South Africa's universities, technikons and community health training centres include study of the traditional healing system and explore areas for collaboration. South Africa's Medicines Control Council (MCC) commissioned a study by the University of Cape Town's Traditional Medicines Programme (Tramed.) Tramed travelled to Washington DC to review the international regulatory scene and now, the MCC is considering adopting the study's recommendations as policy.

The traditional healers I interviewed freely admitted that, in certain cases, modern medicine is preferable and can cure diseases they cannot. They believe, for instance, that as yet there is no cure for Aids. They regularly refer their patients to clinics for blood testing and lab work. I found these healers curious about new treatments and therapies. They often approach medical professionals in their district and assimilate into their own practice any available techniques that seem to work. The traditional healers seem to integrate new knowledge with their own culture of healing, something no outsider can do for them. One challenge to the modern health system, therefore, is to make new scientific information and technology more accessible to the traditional healers.

The traditional healers form a crucial link between the community and the western medical professionals. Senior, credible traditional healers are well-established, well-respected, accepted and trusted by the community. They are a precious resource for the dissemination of basic health care, especially in rural areas where access to information is limited. They are readily available after hours when the already scarce local health services are not functioning. They also meet urgent but often under-funded needs, such as patient counselling, family support and home visits.

The traditional healers I visited have no doubts as to either the legitimacy or the efficacy of their healing. Traditional healing is a deep-rooted part of African life and, the traditional healers believe, will continue as long as African culture survives. Approximately 200 000 strong in South Africa alone, consulting to eighty per cent of the general population, clearly the traditional healers are here to stay.

In my early contact with the sangomas of Swaziland, I saw medicinal plants, barks and herbs being pulverised into powder form and stored in clean glass bottles. I witnessed sangomas taking pains to gather or purchase herbs from areas not contaminated by pesticides. The purity of the herb was crucial. I learned that herbal medicine could be administered in a variety of ways. The powdered form of the herb could be boiled and taken as a tea. It could be inhaled during a simple steaming process such as one might use when easing the congestion of a common cold. The herbal powder could be rubbed lightly into a shallow cut (a superficial incision like a paper cut) called a 'traditional injection'. Being an American and used to a high standard of medical hygiene, I was immediately concerned about the spread of HIV/Aids and other infectious diseases. I wondered how or if the healers kept their practices and their patients safe, but was reassured, on my first site visits, to see surgical gloves and disposable sterilised razor blades (provided by the government health department) in use.

Having grown up with images gleaned from Hollywood films and *National Geographic* magazines, I had assumed African healers would be quite mysterious and visualised them operating in an almost fetishistic setting. The reality could not have been further from the truth. In rural huts and at modern urban traditional clinics, I was invited to examine the various traditional healing tools and objects. There were such things as sticks, gourds and bowls for mixing medicines; shells in which to burn herbs, incense-like; pestle and mortar for grinding the herbs. Each object had a use in the healer's practice but not one was believed to have magical powers to cure disease. Traditional clothing or fabric used in healing ceremonies was often hung colourfully in one area of the room. Animal skins or mats were laid out on well-swept and polished floors where the patient could sit comfortably. The traditional healer's training certificates were displayed alongside informative Department of Health posters, the same posters seen in government clinics. File cards were kept on current and past patients complete with diagnosis, treatment, referral made and follow-up.

In the traditional clinics I visited, many healers had a small area dedicated to their ancestors. The area might have a small sculpture or even a wooden image representing the ancestor, or perhaps something the ancestor was fond of when alive. Here the sangomas would greet their ancestors in a prayer-like fashion before beginning the consultation. I innocently asked about these sculptures and images. Were they in fact making a kind of devotion to the objects themselves? The sangomas found the idea of attributing praise or power to an inanimate object quite amusing. Their objects, they explained, were simply representations, placed out of respect, to honour the spirit of their beloved ancestors. One sangoma, also a Roman Catholic, compared the objects to statues in her church: 'When praying in front of, or placing flowers at the likeness of Mother Mary, I do not think for one minute that the statue has any particular power, but it helps me remember Jesus' mother. I am not giving devotion to the likeness but to the spirit of Mother Mary.'

Another of my stereotypes was challenged by an elderly sangoma. I had travelled to a rural area of Swaziland to meet a traditional healer famous for her ability to 'change luck'. So many of my misconceptions about superstitious healers spouting mumbo jumbo had been shattered – but this promised to be different. Changing luck? What kind of tricks was she playing on her patients? I was anxious to see.

The healer, when I challenged her, let out a huge laugh, patted my hand as if I were a naïve child, and told me this story. 'A patient, an African man about forty years old, came to see me from the city, from Mbabane. This man was very frustrated. Several times he had been passed up for promotion by his boss. He wanted to have his "luck changed". I told him, "Go back to your work. Tell your boss you must come to me for treatment for one week. You are not well. Do not worry. He will not fight you. You will be surprised by his understanding."'

The following week, this man returned to the traditional clinic. The healer prepared a room for him and asked him to rest and sleep. For three days he felt exhausted. He didn't read, listen to the radio or even converse much. He began to relax. The healer fed him only soup broth and herbal teas. After three days she served some strained but not yet solid foods. The patient began to feel a desire to exercise and he enjoyed long walks among the homesteads and along the quiet dirt roads. At the end of the week's 'treatment', he was no longer feeling anxious and was eager to return to his family in the city. The healer said, 'When you return to work, continue this healthy diet and your walking exercise. Try to stay calm as you are now and have patience with those around you. Come back to see me in two weeks' time. Then we will talk about your "luck".'

Two weeks passed and the patient returned to the sangoma. 'You have changed my luck!' he said. 'When I returned to my job I saw clearly how bored and tired I was with my work. I decided it was not my boss's fault that I was unhappy. I told my friends and soon they were bringing job notices to my attention. I started a new job last week and it suits me perfectly. I was able to leave my old job with no hard feelings. My boss was full of understanding and quite glad to see me go. I was not a happy employee for him.'

The sangoma explained to the patient, 'When you moved to the city, you lost the healthy rhythm of exercise and eating natural foods that was taken for granted in your rural life. You became unbalanced in your body and in your spirit. In the city, you sat in a chair or drove a car, but did not walk. You drank coffee rather than rested when you were tired. You became toxic, confused, and began to blame others for your unhappiness and misfortune. You turned your back on your ancestors – and so they brought you to me. I did not change your luck! You changed your own luck. And what is this 'luck'? It is an ability to see clearly what is in front of us. It is the strength to take responsibility for our own actions. When can we do this? Only when our bodies and minds are healthy.'

Traditional African medicine and treatments address healing of both the body and the spirit and can be a catalyst for subtle yet profound changes, such as in the patient looking to 'change his luck'. These healers seemed in perfect sync with current research and thought on spiritual health. Indigenous spiritual traditions from Europe, Asia, America and Africa, for example, are being studied in psychology institutes across the USA today as the public demonstrates an increasing interest in the healing power of these ancient practices. Some Americans who have lost touch with the spiritual traditions of their own ancestry, or become disillusioned with modern religious institutions, have turned to the healing rituals of the Native American Indian tribes. In the USA, Native American Indians were banned from performing certain traditional ceremonies until as recently as the 1970s. Today, there is a growing resurgence of healing rituals – such as the sweat lodge, a sacred group therapy practice. The sweat lodge is being used increasingly by psychologists, therapists and counsellors working with patients in the area of alcohol and substance abuse. The Native American Medicine Man, or traditional healer, is working side by side with western trained psychologists in hospitals and treatment facilities, especially in the south western and western United States.

Several years ago, the Traditional Healers Organisation for Africa was visited in southern Africa by a small group of Native American Indian healers. The sangomas were touched by an instant connection they felt with the Indians. The similarities between their healing traditions and music were striking. Their understanding of the ancestors ran parallel. A shared intent to reintroduce traditional spirituality to their younger generations was deeply discussed. Some argue that all indigenous healing shares a basic tradition at the root. I certainly witnessed a striking camaraderie between the African sangomas and healers of other traditions.

Beyond the common philosophies and some similarities in herbal treatments, I found the healers had an uncanny ability to communicate and share information across great distances – even international borders – without the benefit of telephones, fax machines or other technology and services we take for granted in the modern world. I had often heard the traditional healers referred to as primitive, uneducated or even unworldly. International visitors and western-educated Africans often dismissed the sangoma even before introductions were made. This usually happened as we entered the rustic homesteads. How 'gifted and bright' could anyone be, given these poor surroundings? One such incident brought me to the limit of my patience and highlighted this global interconnectedness of which I speak.

One evening I was preparing for an early morning trip to the bush to visit the Zulu healer, PH Mntshali, when I received a phone call from a neighbour. She had an overseas holiday guest quite keen on traditional healing. Would I be willing to take her with me on this trip? The visitor turned out to be a European consultant, who had lived and worked for years in China. Asian traditional medicine had helped her prevent surgery and successfully controlled her chronic pain. Impressed by these results, the woman began studying under a Chinese Qigong or Qi Master. In oriental traditional medicine, Qi is the animating force that allows us to function, move, think and feel. This Qi circulates along pathways that link together all parts of the human body. If blocked, a person can experience physical, mental and spiritual illness. I found her knowledgeable and stimulating. We made a plan to travel together the following day. I was pleased to be bringing PH Mntshali a visitor from another medical tradition.

The next day we travelled several hours to the healer's homestead near Siteki, Swaziland. The visitor settled comfortably on the mats in his hut. We had a brief discussion about oriental medicine, then, since Mntshali's time was short that day, we quickly moved on to an interview he had promised me. The subject of divining 'bones' arose, and he told us how he had come to acquire his own set.

Coached only by his ancestors in dreams and visions for fifteen years,

Mntshali had developed an impressive breadth and depth of healing knowledge. During this time a North African man came to live nearby. From a healing tradition himself, this man recognised Mntshali's ability and suggested that he use a diagnostic tool. He made a gift to Mntshali of a set of domino-like carved wooden pieces. To demonstrate their use, Mntshali threw them on the floor next to my feet and began to interpret their meaning. He said he did not want to offend the visitor as she had not asked for a consultation, but the ancestors had pointed the pieces directly at her. Mntshali and I agreed that he would throw the pieces again, reminding the ancestors that this diagnosis was for me, not the visitor, who had reacted negatively to the idea of a consultation.

The pieces were thrown randomly and again they pointed to the woman. Mntshali was quiet for a moment, then said, 'I am sorry, madam, but the ancestors wish me to tell you something. I think this may be uncomfortable but I must do as I am asked. Mrs Campbell may leave now if you wish some privacy.'

The visitor asked me to stay and agreed to hear Mntshali speak. What came next was disturbing.

'Madam, you have an important ancestor trying very hard to reach and help you,' Mntshali began. 'He is an older man who was not good to you in his life. He feels great sorrow and remorse now. He wishes to heal the past and your wounds. This ancestor is your father's brother.'

The woman was speechless. Suddenly she challenged Mntshali. How could he know anything? He lived in a remote, undeveloped area. He had not studied for years in a highly sophisticated system like the Asians. The Orient was a place of high culture, not primitive like Africa. This consultation was ridiculous and had even given her a headache!

'A headache?' Mntshali asked.

'Yes,' she said, 'and in China I would use a special oil from my Qi doctor which would alleviate my headache instantly. Now I must just suffer.'

Mntshali said he knew of this medicine and in fact had some in his supply hut. He left to fetch it for her.

In his absence, the visitor was agitated and distressed. She ridiculed Mntshali and African healers in general. I apologised for the discomfort she was experiencing but said I could not allow her to be disrespectful to this important healer. I told her we would leave as soon as Mntshali returned.

Mntshali entered the clinic hut with a lovely smile on his face and handed a small bottle to the woman. She looked at the Chinese writing and opened the oil to smell. Her face registered shock as she applied her 'special' headache oil. Mntshali explained that some years ago a Chinese Qi doctor came to visit him. They had a rewarding time together. For days they exchanged a wealth of information and examined their healing successes and challenges.

'How did a Chinese doctor end up in Swaziland? How did he find you?' the woman asked.

'How does anyone find another? Mntshali asked. 'How did Mrs Campbell find the healers in Africa? How did you find Mrs Campbell? How is it you are in Africa when Asia is your passion? Do you think this is all by accident? No, it is our ancestors guiding us, of course,' and he gave out such a heartfelt laugh.

The visitor, already feeling the calming effects of the oil, explained that she had recently been transferred to a job in Egypt. She missed her Qi doctor. There were no Chinese people in her neighbourhood. Mntshali said, 'Not to worry. This ancestor of yours, this very old man, is going to fix that.'

We said our good-byes and headed back towards home. The woman was tired and slept peacefully for much of the trip. I heard later she returned safely to North Africa and was busy with her new assignment. A fortnight later I received an unexpected and beautiful fax from her. It seems that the ancestor Mntshali referred to in the consultation was the very man who sexually abused her as a child. The memories and hurt had stayed buried until just days before visiting Mntshali. At 39 years old, memories and dreams began flooding back. Terribly upset by the consultation, she returned to Cairo wondering why God would revive her painful past without even the help of the traditional medicine system she had come to trust and rely on. Returning to her office in a depressed and worried state, she opened the blinds to her window and looked down below at the street scene and saw an amazing sight. Across the road was an older Chinese man hanging a sign, 'Chinese Qi Master'. Her ancestors continued to provide for her as the Chinese doctor helped her process and resolve her pain.

There are many stories which highlight the spiritual contact the African healers have in the world, despite their physical or financial limitations. PH Mntshali visited the States for the first time in 1995. He had predicted this visit, based on prior dreams, and also said that I would meet an American doctor in Washington, DC, who, like himself, was trying to help his patients make contact with their ancestors. I would help Mntshali meet this doctor.

True to Mntshali's predictions, I met Dr Ray Moody at a presentation on mind–body medicine given by the Smithsonian Institute. Dr Moody, I learned, was famous for his research on near-death experiences and had been working with a method to help patients make direct contact with loved ones who had passed away, their 'ancestors'. The technique, described in his book Reunions, often brought healing to those who participated. During his trip to the States, Mntshali spent a week at Dr Moody's Mind Body Institute in Alabama. The only indigenous healer among a group of prominent physicians, Mntshali was a great success as he shared his perspective and experience. 'In such a rich and learned place as America,' he said, 'I was surprised my ancestors had so much to teach these medical doctors. So many people had forgotten their ancestors and neglected their calling. There is much we can share from Africa.'

While Mntshali was in the States, I was setting up house in Warsaw, Poland. I felt extremely distant from Africa in this new culture and climate. Ninety-nine per cent of the people were white, spoke Polish and belonged to the Catholic Church. I was in a one-tribe country. I struggled with my survival Polish and was challenged to receive a smile from anyone on the streets. One day my family and I were strolling through Warsaw's beautiful old town area when we spotted a tall, black man. He looked over at us and smiled. We walked over and chatted. A pharmacy student from Kenya, the young man had just completed two years in intensive language school. The next several years would be spent learning medical terms in Polish. We commiserated over missing Africa but consoled each other with the tremendous opportunity to experience this part of the world as it transitioned from decades of communism.

While in Warsaw, I was invited to speak to the Polish Society for Natural Medicine. This group of mature physicians, scientists and natural healers promote cooperation between western medical and complementary healing practitioners. I was to speak, through an interpreter, about my experience with African traditional healers. I was quite excited that such interest existed and organised my best slides for the presentation. My Polish interpreter had spent some time in northern Africa and had a love for the continent. She had worked with me on other occasions and I was confident she would relay my words and sentiment accurately.

The presentation was followed by an hour of questions from the audience. There was genuine interest in the African healers. Some weeks later I was approached by a journalist who had been at my talk and wanted to interview me for a popular Polish magazine which covered alternative healing issues. Her managing editor had said he did not think an article about Africa would capture their readers' attention. She was free to do the interview – but, he warned her, the public would not be interested. Africa was just too foreign to Poles.

After reading the interview and deciding to run the article (well hidden in an issue), the managing editor had a change of heart: to the journalist's surprise the article appeared as a feature story in September 1995. She was all the more perplexed as the September edition had historically been their largest seller. Why would he take a chance? As it turned out, the issue sold out and even needed reprinting. I posted copies, with an English translation, to the sangomas I had met in southern Africa. Their stories and their images had touched the hearts of doctors and healers they would later meet.

In August 1996, while I was in the Eastern Cape of South Africa, sangomas told me that they had seen a spiritual leader in a dream. This was a holy man important to the world who was from the East. He would be 'welcomed by Africans because his smile and laughter, his love for humanity is like that of a father. He reminds us of our Madiba (President Mandela) and Bishop Tutu. He can forgive hard things. When you get back to Johannesburg you will see in the newspapers who he is. When you move back to America, you will have some chances to learn about this man's spiritual and healing traditions. You will enjoy this and even bring some of us to America to meet with these healers from the East.' I found this interesting, as none of these healers, when probed, had expressed any knowledge of or exposure to spiritual or healing traditions of Asia. I remembered Mntshali's unusual visit by the Chinese doctor, however, and did not discount the dream.

Upon my return to Johannesburg, I found the local newspaper, *The Star*, on my kitchen table. On the front page was a photo of His Holiness, the Dalai Lama. Unbeknown to me, the exiled head of state and spiritual leader of the Tibetan people had visited South Africa. I had always admired his compassion and found his writings inspirational. Now perhaps there was something more to be learned, something about Tibetan Buddhism and its traditional medicine. I didn't see an immediate fit with my present plans but I knew how things can change.

In June 1997, Swazi healer Khumbulile Mdluli and Dr Richard

Lemmer, a South African physician, travelled to Boulder, Colorado to speak at an international conference of healers, medical practitioners and scientists. I was unable to attend due to prior commitments in South Africa. Dr Stefania Szantyr-Powolny, a distinguished Polish healer and medical doctor, member of the board of directors of the Polish Society for Natural Medicine and a close colleague of mine from Warsaw, was also at that conference. Khumbulile, through her traditional consultations in Africa, had led me to Dr Szantyr-Powolny and the Wirkus Foundation which co-sponsored the conference. Khumbulile had never been outside southern Africa. She had no telephone, read no international newspapers or scientific journals, yet she had made several important international connections through her traditional healing and divining practises.

At that same conference was a Tibetan Buddhist Traditional Doctor, Dr Dickey Nyerongsha, recently arrived in the USA from Dharmsala, India, the Dalai Lama's home in exile. A sixth-generation traditional doctor, she offered much insight and enjoyed meeting the international participants. A year later I returned to the States to pursue further university studies in southern California. Much to my surprise, I learned that a Dr Dickey Nyerongsha would be lecturing in Tibetan medicine in my Ph.D. psychology programme. Was this a coincidence? Dr Nyerongsha and I both thought not, as I relayed the dreams of the Transkei sangomas and she remembered Khumbulile Mdluli fondly from the past year's conference.

In June 1998, I had an opportunity to meet my colleague Sharon Corsaro's teacher, Ruben Orellana, visiting from Peru. Ruben, a western educated and oriented man, much like the sangomas in this book, had answered a call to traditional healing. He was drawn to the practices and philosophies of the ancient Incan civilisation while he was head of archaeology at Machu Pichuu, where he discovered 44 new archeological sites surrounding this holy city in South America. As Sharon told me of Ruben, I remembered incidents with the African healers that involved Peru.

While in Africa, Mntshali had once told me that I would find a story set in Peru, 'like a teaching story or a fable', that would become very popular. It would be a good healing story. I would learn about the book while in the States. When it was brought to my attention, I should post a copy to him. While temporarily in Washington, DC, waiting with my family to depart for our assignment in Poland, I received a phone call from a local bookshop owner. He said, 'Susan, I just bought some books from a guy selling them from his car. He published the book himself and I've only one left. It's a good story, set in Peru. I think you'd like it. I'll save it for you.' I bought the book, read it quickly and posted it to Mntshali. I later learned that the rights to the book had been bought by Time Warner, the American media and publishing conglomerate. *The Celestine Prophecy* became a huge seller and the author, James Redfield, no longer had to sell books from his car.

Several years later I was back in southern Africa, meeting the Sanusi (highest level of healer in the Zulu tradition) Credo Vusa'mazula Mutwa. It was quite an honour to meet Credo, especially as he was departing for Peru the next day to attend a small, exclusive gathering of international indigenous healers. There was tremendous pressure on his time and I appreciated his fitting me in. He was very gentle and kind, though not looking forward to his arduous travel ahead. I gave him my necklace of unpolished Baltic Sea amber which, according to Polish healing tradition, has properties to calm and soothe. Credo talked about the camaraderie of native healers the world over and encouraged me to persevere with my efforts to bring African healers into contact with their international counterparts, especially those in the Americas. Credo remembered his contemporary and friend, PH Mntshali, and blessed my work on *Called to Heal*.

With these stories in mind, I grabbed a photo of Credo and one of Mntshali to bring to my lunch meeting with the healer and archaeologist, Ruben Orellana. The meeting was a delight and lasted long after the lunch hour. I showed Ruben my photos and he said, 'Of course. I was with Credo Mutwa in Peru for an international healers' gathering. He taught and led powerful healings for us. He was having some difficulty with the altitude, though, and I gave a healing ceremony for him. And this man (pointing to Mntshali), this is the Zulu healer Credo is so very fond of.' My colleague looked in disbelief and said, 'What are the chances of Ruben knowing these Africans, Susan? He has no orientation to that part of the world. How is it possible?'

Chances? Accidents? Credo, Mntshali, Ruben and the sangomas would say not.

Part One:
My Journey

1

My own journey towards the healers

My time in Swaziland proved important orientation for the work I would later do in the region. I would like to share a bit of this 'mother experience', as the Swazi sangomas called it, before telling the healers' own stories. Like many western-educated Africans and Europeans, I considered traditional healers part of a primitive – and very foreign – cultural past. I did not encounter traditional healers in my management advising work in Africa and did not think of them as professionals, if I thought of them at all.

In 1991, I was vice-president of Bank of America's largest subsidiary in the United States when my husband was asked to consider a two-year assignment in Swaziland, southern Africa. Ron and I had visited the Kingdom of Swaziland in 1983 and remembered it as beautiful, mountainous, green. We thought our son would enjoy the easy nature of the Swazis and love the access to nature, after our fast-paced urban life. For me to make the move, though, I needed substantive work. I explored a return to private consulting, which I had done years earlier, before our son was born. To test the waters, I visited potential clients in Washington, DC and was received warmly. Our decision was a 'go'. I felt focused and knew exactly what I would be doing in Africa. I had no idea that by the end of my time in Swaziland, I would be turning down lucrative consulting opportunities to honour my schedule with African traditional healers.

I wondered whether Swaziland would be too much like America, especially living in Mbabane, the capital city, with a population of 60 000 people. Were the towns too westernised, the cultural differences too subtle to challenge our son? I needn't have worried. Joseph, our four-year-old, talked non-stop during the twenty minute shuttle from the Manzini airport. 'Those ladies are carrying wood on their heads. Why is everyone barefoot? I don't have to wear shoes here. The houses are round. That roof is made of grass. Watch out for the donkeys!' On that short ride, my concerns evaporated.

Ron and I had lived in Africa and the South Pacific. We were familiar with the hundreds of adjustments that take place in those first few months, but had never undertaken them with a child. What was our health care and emergency support system to be? What was the school situation for Joseph? Where would we shop – and was there anything in the shops? How would we get around: were taxis and buses dependable? We discovered on-again, off-again electricity, water and phone services, as well as a postal system that seemed to function on the whim of its counter staff. Our personal effects freight arrived with half the boxes broken into. Fortunately, these inconveniences came one by one and were never to overwhelm us.

Surrounded on three sides by South Africa and on the east by Mozambique, Swaziland is a small country, only slightly larger than Hawaii. Just under a million people, the majority members of the Swazi tribe, live on approximately 6 700 square miles of land. The national language is siSwati but English is the language of commerce and is taught in the primary schools. The Swazi life, like that of most rural southern Africans, remains a physically strenuous one. There is no electricity or running water in most rural areas. People walk miles to carry water back from their nearest source. When the parents can afford the tuition fees, the children go to school. After school, the children help with the cattle, cooking, laundry and care of younger siblings as well as catering to the elderly in their extended families.

Women of all ages carry babies on their backs to free both hands (and their heads) for carrying other things. The most impressive balancing act I saw was a woman walking through town during the rainy season carrying a large, upright vacuum cleaner on her head. It was perfectly balanced and never even threatened to fall off as she traversed rocky, slippery terrain in unpredictable automobile traffic. In addition to shopping parcels and baskets, I've seen women carry sewing machines and ten gallon gasoline containers on their heads. Swaziland is a patriarchal society, and polygamy is still practised. Many of the healers, like their counterparts throughout the region, believe that polygamy has outlived its original purposes, including protection of the women during tribal wars.

During our first few weeks I decided to be a tourist and enjoy whatever Swaziland had to offer. Joseph was unable to start school for three months so he had a holiday to write home about. We explored the capital, Mbabane, starting with the public markets. Joseph is blond, fair-skinned and tall for his age. Swazis were greeting him, touching his hair, asking him hundreds of questions. I realised then that being back in Africa with a child was a whole different experience. With Joseph, we were in an accelerated experiential mode, making mistakes, getting laughed at but learning quickly.

After we figured out how and where to obtain the basics to survive comfortably, we looked towards nature. Joseph and I headed out to visit our first Swazi game park, less than ten miles from Mbabane, the Mlil-wane Wildlife Sanctuary. We were thrilled with Mlilwane, an 11 125 acre game and nature reserve with altitudes ranging from 2 100 to 4 700 feet. The park, including a rest camp with thatched wooden and traditional grass beehive huts, is still rustic and uncommercialised. The roads are dirt and require a four-wheel drive for the more adventurous routes. We had our little Ford Escort, which we had purchased quickly to get ourselves mobile.

The Swazi ranger guarding the entrance to the park told us that Mlilwane had a variety of animals, including white rhino, zebra, kudu, impala, springbok, hippo, giraffe, warthog, waterbuck, crocodile and vervet monkey, to name a few. We couldn't wait to see just one or two of these animals. We drove slowly with many, many stops as we sighted game. Joseph perched up on the passenger door, window rolled down, holding onto the roof of the car. This was as close as he could get to the animals without getting out of the car, which was not allowed. We were so caught up in the beauty of the park and the animals that I hadn't noticed it was getting very hot, approaching noon. It struck me that I hadn't seen another car or other human being in the four hours we had been wandering around.

The heat was oppressive and we had no food or water. Joseph was madly pointing at something. I turned and saw a giraffe looking down at us from my side of the car. I looked into the animal's eye and felt hypnotised. For a second I saw a picture reflected in his eyeball of Joseph and myself stranded in the park. It happened so fast and was so strange, I discounted it as a reaction to the heat. Two minutes later, our car engine died. There wasn't much breeze and we were melting. An hour passed with no help in sight.

I decided we would walk back to the ranger's hut. I gave Joseph a big hug. I didn't mean to, but I cried. I wasn't sure if there were lions in the park (there were not) and I was uncertain how I would keep Joseph safe. I felt badly that I had gotten him into this mess just a few weeks into his first African experience. Joseph patted me on the back and gave me a hug. We started walking. It was so incredibly quiet and beautiful. We turned a corner and were greeted by a family of warthogs. I had heard they could be quite vicious and asked Joseph to be very quiet and still. We edged on by while they dug at the ground and snorted at us. So far, so good.

The heat would not let up. Most of the animals were resting under the shade trees. Joseph's feet were aching and the heat was too much for him. I couldn't carry him far and wondered how we were going to make it out of the park. We walked five miles before we saw a car. A family of three Zimbabweans stopped and offered us water. We collapsed in their back seat, dusty, sweaty and ever so grateful. We were closer to a main road than to a ranger station so we agreed to be dropped off at a nearby hotel. As we pulled up to the Happy Valley Hotel, I realised we had landed in Mbabane's red light district. Fortunately it was early afternoon and the trade for the strip-tease performances and pornographic films was slim. I managed to keep Joseph at my side, not an easy task when he discovered video games with graphics unlike any he'd seen before.

A receptionist at the front desk offered to ring Ron, who found a 'bush' mechanic and came to rescue us. We had one more tour of the park as I tried to remember where we had left the car. The terrain all looked the same to me. Had we turned at this shrub? At that thornbush? We found the car. The problem turned out to be a loose connection with the battery cables. That evening our discussions of the benefits of having a solid four-wheel-drive vehicle gained momentum.

Joseph and I continued to venture further and further out, though what was to be one of our favourite parks – Malolotja Park, in the mountainous highveld – was close to home. Malolotja is Swaziland's largest wildlife park and is a haven for hikers. The park encourages game and bird viewing by foot. By this time we had figured out how to hike safely among the wildlife and discovered some small log cabins for overnight stays. We would wake up to a herd of forty or so blesbuck in our front 'yard'. This time was an amazing gift, one of many I was to receive from this part of the world.

In February 1992, my family and I celebrated my fortieth birthday, African style, with a glorious weekend in the bush. As a surprise, Ron had tried to arrange a visit to a traditional healer's homestead – a one-time-only experience, a welcome respite from our urban work. The nature reserve had been unable to arrange the visit, but had given Ron the name of 'Dr' Nhlavana Maseko, who could make a referral for us and recommend a day trip to visit a healer.

The note with Maseko's name on it sat in my wallet for three months. During those months an odd thing happened. I began to feel dissatisfied with my work. There was always something not quite right in everything I did or considered doing. I couldn't understand this and it annoyed me. Getting a phone installed in Mbabane can take years and while we were waiting for ours, my neighbour, Paige, offered the convenient use of her phone. One day while catching up on phone calls, I began having this strong thought, 'call the healer', over and over again. I finally told Paige, who said: 'That sounds like fun. Let's do it. Call him now.' Her enthusiasm was infectious. I fished out the phone number from my wallet and dialled.

A voice on the phone said: 'Hello, this is THO (The Traditional Healers Organisation for Africa).' I asked to speak with Dr Maseko and my call passed to a man who questioned my purpose. I explained, 'I am an American consultant living in Swaziland. I would like to visit a traditional healer. My work keeps me in cities and I thought this might be one way to learn more about Swazi traditional life.' He responded with a gruff: 'Who gave you Dr Maseko's name?' I wondered just who Dr Maseko was. Was it poor protocol to phone him like this? I tried searching for a way to gracefully disengage until I had more information. Lost in my anxious thoughts, I heard: 'Hello, Mrs Campbell, this is Dr Maseko.' Thanking him for taking my call, I said I would like to meet him.

At this point I felt like an observer to my own actions, a sensation to be repeated often in the coming months. I had intended simply to ask him for a referral to a healer in my vicinity, but Dr Maseko asked, 'Can you drive up here tomorrow? We are at Siteki, less than a two-hour drive from Mbabane.' Without hesitation, we set an appointment. I didn't know why I was doing this, but I sensed it would be fun – and that I could use a day off.

The following day I drove to Siteki. I enjoyed the scenic ride out of the mountains through Swaziland's dry lowveld, up onto a plateau, close to the Mozambique border. It was so different, so beautiful and very soothing. I stopped in Siteki to ask for help with directions. Finally, I arrived at an old hotel with a THO sign on it. The hotel was small and western in style with an addition of new traditional rondavels. There was plenty of activity, staff people in western dress scurrying about with papers. A conference room was busy with a training workshop or meeting of some sort. It felt very professional.

I spotted a reception building. As I walked towards it, I was greeted by Betty, the THO receptionist. She told me that Dr Maseko had had some anxious thoughts himself. He did not know who I was and could not meet with me. It was unusual for him even to have suggested it on the phone. Betty conveyed his apologies.

My heart sank. Pulling together my diplomatic skills, I explained how I came to have Dr Maseko's name, but I was getting nowhere. What if I were to obtain a letter of introduction? Dr Maseko could then decide if I was someone he wished to meet. It occurred to me that I was being provided an escape route and I prepared to leave. Suddenly the phone rang and Betty asked me to wait. She answered the phone, listened intently, said 'Yes' then hung up. She looked baffled. 'Dr Maseko will see you,' she said. 'Please come this way.' I followed Betty down a short hall. As she was about to knock on the door she told me that several times a year Dr Maseko called together his senior healers. It just happened that they were here today and I would be meeting with them as well. I felt my stomach turn. I had a slow-motion sensation of jumping off a cliff with no safety net.

There were shoes outside the door and I wondered if I should take my dress shoes off. Before I could decide I was led into a room where Dr Maseko, a distinguished looking older gentleman, held court. I noticed he had an animal skin hanging from his waist over the traditional Swazi cloth. He wore a feather in a leopard skin circling his head. We shook hands and greeted one another.

r Maseko welcomed me on behalf of THO and the healers. I noticed that several women were seated on the floor. They had striking hair coloured with red ochre, a mud dye, and braided with beads. Their faces were beautiful, their smiles radiant. Their presence was strong. Some of the men had feathers in their hair and were also wearing fur and animal skins. One older man caught my eye. He smiled and his face lit up. I felt myself relaxing just making eye contact with him.

Dr Maseko told me a little about their organisation. I was surprised by its size and international membership. I was disorientated by the look of these people. In my navy business suit, I felt I had just stepped into a different world. I had never seen an African traditional healer before, yet I felt no distance between us. They were so kind and comfortable. I was caught up in the experience. I was an observer yet I was no longer wondering what I was doing there. I was thoroughly enjoying the moment.

Dr Maseko asked me to explain who I was and my interest in their group. I looked at the older man with the electric smile and received a thought: 'Tell them about your banking experience.' The mental suggestion was so strong, I felt this man had been talking to me. Yet the room was silent. He had not spoken a word. I proceeded to talk about my banking experience in Seattle. They were interested. I heard myself telling the story of Dick Cooley, former Chief Executive Officer of Wells Fargo Bank in California, being approached by Seafirst Bank on the cusp of his retirement to turn this corporation around. Arriving in Seattle, he was surprised at how bad the situation really was. The bank had taken a dive, gone beyond its expertise into energy loans. The bottom had fallen out of the oil industry, Seafirst was going down fast. It had plenty of company across the USA but that was no consolation. Dick had to make hard changes fast.

A voice said, 'Tell them about alcohol and exercise.'

'Oh yes, good idea,' I exclaimed, then looked around the room and noticed fleetingly that no one had spoken. It was very quiet.

The healers wanted to hear the rest of the story. Incongruous perhaps, but I launched into stories of Cooley banning alcohol from the bankers' offices, introducing incentives to get people working out, joining health clubs. Dick, a fit and healthy man, lost his right hand during World War II but remained an avid skier and cyclist. This man had challenges, not excuses. There were many policy and procedural changes that altered how lending was done at Seafirst – but I was painting a picture of how Dick Cooley changed the 'spirit' of the bank.

I continued, telling them about my other professional experiences in Washington, DC, the Solomon Islands and Botswana. My personal interest in the intersection of western thought and traditional practice. I had not publicly articulated these thoughts before, yet it seemed so natural.

Three and a half hours passed. No one left the room during our discussion. It felt timeless, as if we had been together only a few minutes. It was so pleasant to be with these healers! The conversation flowed easily.

Then Dr Maseko smiled and said: 'You are a business woman. What do you want from us?'

Without hesitation, I replied: 'I want to write a book about you.'

I was shocked. Where had that thought come from? My intention had been to set up one visit with a traditional healer.

Dr Maseko said: 'Of course, many people want to write about us.'

I thought: 'What an absurd idea, to write a book! When would I have the time? How would I put it together? Who am I to write about the healers?' I felt incredibly foolish. I was embarrassed. Next, I heard myself launching into a sales pitch on why I should write about them. I felt detached, as if I was two people having two separate streams of thought.

I told them about the mixed signals I had received from the media and the medical profession about traditional healers. Are they witch-doctors? How can people order a patient to kill a child, mutilate another human being, steal from others, and call themselves healers?

'Those are witchdoctors, not healers,' explained Dr Maseko. 'Possessed healers, healers with a spiritual calling from the ancestors, cannot harm their patients or others by virtue of their calling. It is important to fight these negative impressions, but THO's main mission is to provide primary health care. Our goals and accomplishments are ambitious. We have no time to set right this confusion. We are here to heal.'

Nevertheless, Dr Maseko and the senior healers invited me to submit a proposal to THO outlining how I would go about creating a book about them. I was pleased but surprised, even startled by my new mission. Dr Maseko later admitted having been surprised at his own behaviour, his own unexpected willingness to accommodate me, to meet with no introduction. He said he felt something pushing him to meet with me, and that this showed 'our working relationship is to be backed by both our spirits'.

The healers at this initial meeting were very spiritual people, with the ability to hear others' thoughts and sense a person's strength of intent and character. They were 'seeing' exactly who I was. PH Mntshali, a prominent master healer, recalls the meeting in his own words: 'I remember your first visit. You came alone. The healers who were there that day thought you were a very brave woman, to come by yourself. You were taking a chance to come among us like that. It made a strong impression. We were prepared to listen to you. At first we could not believe your interest was true but as we were with you we thought: 'The white people do not always have to be the ones that are laughing at us, saying untrue things about us.' Dr Maseko questioned you thoroughly and your answers were sincere. You are a business person. You came to Swaziland on a mission with your husband and family. You happen to be interested to see what is THO and what the healers do in this country. It was of personal interest to you.

'It seemed to us that you could do interviews and say truly what the healers are doing in southern Africa. You have heard stories about traditional healers in Africa but have had no experience with them. You were not a doctor or a scientist or an anthropologist. You were a - layperson come among us. We began to feel that you should have an opportunity to meet some of the healers but we wanted to be sure, as you did, that you met with the right people. It was very good that you approached us in a proper manner. You did not do what many people have done in the past, collecting information at random, even showing our customs, our treatments and ways of healing, out of context so people get a wrong impression. The world is expecting good of us. They are ready now for a true picture.

'Mrs Campbell, you asked many, many questions at the beginning of your project and we clarified some of the mistaken stereotypes of the healers. You were very curious. One question in particular I remember was: 'What is the difference between a witchdoctor and a healer?' You see, many people do not even know there is a difference, but already you wanted it straight in your mind before you started the interviewing process. We were able to sit with you and get it straight in your mind that the healer only cures people, helps people. By the rules of the ancestors who invest power in us, a healer cannot use the right hand to cure a person then use that same hand to kill. If that happens, the power goes away immediately after such a harmful act is commit-ted. The powers to heal are taken away forever.'

I submitted a proposal to THO by fax within five days of that initial meeting. The healers had said, at our first meeting: 'The book you write will be an introduction to healers in the region, but others will come behind and say, "We want to study with these traditional healers." Your book will be a door opening for them. In writing the book and finding someone to publish it, you must just stay open. It will be clear who will help you. In time the book will be published.'

I did not see the healers, Dr Maseko or any of the THO staff for another three months. I was not aware of THO's process during these months, its contact with an international board of trustees, the discussions with the senior healers and THO members. There were days when I completely forgot that I had written the proposal. Then unexpectedly I received a phone call from one of the THO staff members: 'Mrs Campbell, this is Moses. How are you? How is life in Mbabane treating you? I just wanted to say hello.' He talked about their workshops and project activities. I remembered how polite these THO staff members were. I remembered the powerful experience of meeting the healers. I thought again what fun it would be to have the opportunity to spend time with them. Occasionally I answered a few questions for Dr Maseko on my proposal but would then have no contact for weeks. I put the healers to the back of my mind, somewhere behind my 'real' professional life.

Finally, after three months had passed, Ron, Joseph and I were packing up our Land-Rover for a holiday at Cape Vidal, a magical nature reserve on the Indian Ocean. I love the ocean, and the remoteness of this place appealed to me. That day, the healers were far from my mind. Just as we were closing up the truck and the house, a man I had never seen before walked up our driveway. Our house was called the 'caterpillar house' by the Swazis. It was built in the side of a very rocky and rough hill. Every one of its nine levels stretched along the bluff like so many legs. It was a strange looking building from the outside, but built for maximum views of eucalyptus and pine forests. It was a trek up the dirt road to our house and then a sharp incline into the driveway. We didn't often get visitors hiking up to see us.

The Swazi man handed me a manila envelope and said, 'Dr Maseko wanted you to have this.' A signed letter of agreement and a warm note from Dr Maseko let me know he was 'ready to go' as soon as I was. I knew that if this was to be my last time living in Africa, I could not have asked for a better way to spend it. The intensity of my happiness surprised me. We set off in the truck, ready for a vacation to celebrate.

The agreement allowed me to interview the senior healers, assisted by THO headquarters staff. In return for this opportunity, I would design a marketing and public relations strategy for THO and present those findings to potential donors. This would eventually give me a glimpse of the relationship between the medical profession and the traditional healers.

The vast majority of Swazis, regardless of their education, including people with advanced degrees from Europe and the USA, consult traditional healers. I had just been granted access to a wonderful new world.

I have always been told I had 'good intuition' and it seemed to help me in the business world. Working at corporate headquarters in Seattle, I had regular contact with Luke Helms, president of the bank. Luke was a whiz, always ahead of the curve on retail banking services. People said his intuition was sharp and he acted on it. I knew when he asked me for my gut feeling that he wanted that clear, true call on any issue. It was fast and caused me to trust my own instincts. Some in the corporation thought I was crazy to be leaving a growing concern for a 'lark' in Africa. When I said goodbye to Luke, he was excited for me. His parting words were, 'Ignore what people say. I have a feeling that what you are about to do will be more fun than you can imagine.' He was right.

The healers later told me that while I was in Seattle, my ancestors were busy paving the way, preparing for my stay in Swaziland. They say it was no accident that I worked with and met the people I did. It was all opening my mind to the unexpected turn my life would soon take. Both the healers' and my own ancestors had already started working together. At this same time several of the healers were having dreams that an American woman would come to them. Of course they didn't see a banker in high heels and a blue suit, but the outside 'package' never seemed to surprise them.

Initially, I was uneasy telling people about my work with the healers. Several colleagues felt this was not 'serious' work. I often heard the question, 'How are you going to write that up in your resumé?' I was moving in a new direction, but it was not without its growing pains for me and my family.

A turning point came when Ron visited the King of Swaziland to discuss his urban development project. In the meeting the Minister of Housing, Thomas Stephens, was chatting to the King in siSwati, the national language. The King then looked at Ron and said in English, 'So, I understand your wife is doing some work with the traditional healers in Swaziland.' Ron was taken by surprise. He wasn't sure the King would think this was a good thing, was it considered controversial? The King told Ron how important the healers were, that Dr Maseko, with whom I was working, was one of his personal healers. Dr Maseko had also treated his father, King Sobhuza. This encounter elevated the credibility of my project and helped me to understand the importance of drawing a picture of these healers for the public.

One of the first times I took my son out to meet a healer, we visited a well-known medicine or muti specialist. Joseph had always seemed comfortable with my work with the healers and was looking forward to the trip. We met with Mr Sibandze in his muti warehouse. The warehouse resembled a makeshift Quonset hut, made of rounded corrugated iron. The original building had been expanded haphazardly as resources permitted. It was dark inside. Shafts of light from a few small windows spread an almost eerie light on the rows and rows of drying herbs, crocodile and python skins, and other objects used in creating traditional treatments. We stopped to let our eyes adjust.

Joseph walked around looking at everything, asking so many questions. Suddenly he shouted, 'Boy Mom, this is really weird!' I remember wishing I could sink into a deep hole and disappear. I worried that he had offended this important healer who was so graciously showing us things few westerners get to see. Mr Sibandze laughed. He praised Joseph's candid comments. I learned that day that children enjoy a special place in the healers' hearts, as they believe children are much closer than adults to the ancestors' world.

I am not a patient person, nor a particularly rugged individual, yet so much of my work with the healers caused me to drive long distances on rough roads in uncomfortable conditions and wait long periods in huts sitting on mud and dung floors. There was so much waiting. It was not unusual to arrive at a healer's home after several gruelling hours of driving only to find they had been called off to see a patient. There was never any certainty that I would actually make contact. That was extraordinary for me. After going back repeatedly to find the person for the interview, the healer would eventually walk into the homestead and I would instantly feel vibrant. It was energising to be in their presence.

Inevitably, I would feel irritable and impatient for a few days following a healer site visit. I was especially annoyed when I had to run errands, see to ordinary everyday business details or make small talk with acquaintances. I didn't want to be back. I wanted more of the serenity I was feeling in the huts with the traditional healers. As time went on, I found I could spend much more time with the healers and more rapidly make the transition back to my day-to-day world with friends and family. There was some sort of learning and adjustment curve I had to master.

During the three months I waited for THO to reach a final agreement on the book project, I seemed to meet people who had had horrible experiences with healers, people who confused the witchdoctor with the true healer. People were frightened for me and told me so. I was told I would mistakenly be led to witchdoctors. I would suffer great physical and emotional pain. My heart said it would be safe, but would it be? On my first visit to a healer, when my interpreters reminded me of the name of the person I was to meet – an important man and considered very senior among the master healers – everything about the healers suddenly seemed so foreign. Maybe all those naysayers were right, I was out of my element. I was nervous and my stomach was upset. We reached the homestead and out walked PH Mntshali, or PH for short, the fellow I had instantly connected with in the initial meeting. He and his wife greeted us. I felt so good. As soon as I saw PH's face I began to relax. PH's homestead is in dry flat land surrounded by low, scrub brush. We sat in the warm winter sun on mats and listened to the sound of bells tinkling from the goats wandering around outside the fence. I felt myself calming down. The homestead was spotless and the ground had just been swept. The place was picture perfect, as it would be every time I returned.

I didn't appreciate the significance of where we sat that day. PH was keeping me at bay, keeping me a safe distance from his holy places. He asked very sharp and pointed questions about my intent, my background, and my interest in the healers. I remember thinking, 'He's not going to let me interview him. This is my first and last interview.' It was presumptuous on my part to think I could come in and probe into these peoples' lives. Then the mood changed. We did an interview of several hours and it was wonderful. After that experience, we were always to visit inside the huts where he made contact with his ancestors, his sacred traditional healing huts.

PH had been interviewed over the years by many researchers but had seen no published work come of it. He was no longer giving interviews. However, a dream told him my effort would be different. Throughout my experience with the healers, PH was instrumental in helping me. After that visit, I was never interrogated again. I was later told that Dr Maseko and PH had tested and judged my trustworthiness. Dr Maseko then relayed the message to the healers by radio, through meetings and at workshops, that my intentions were pure.

During my time in Swaziland I had an opportunity to spend seven days relaxing at the St Francis Health Spa in Port Alfred, South Africa. At the centre, I had completed a week of fasting, massage and herbal treatments. On the first day of fasting I was quite ill. I only craved silence and sleep. After the third day, I began to get my energy back and see colours, hear sounds, smell smells more vividly. I noticed several emotional issues were completely resolved during this intensified stay. I believed in the mind-body connection but now I had felt it. Here, in action at a European-type spa, were principles the African healers had discussed.

Khumbulile Mdluli, another healer who, like PH, seemed to be tuned into a special wavelength when it came to my well-being, called upon my return. She had no phone of her own but managed to find one when she needed to be in touch. I had no opportunity to speak with Khumbulile before leaving so she didn't know I had been out of the country. Khumbulile told me that she had experienced seven consecutive days of dreams about me. In the dreams I was making a passage. For the first three nights she was not sure whether I was well. The dates of those dreams correlated with the first three days of my fasting. Something then changed in her dreams. It was as if I had moved on. She saw a spiritual passage. She said she was pleased to be 'with' me at the health centre.

The week before I left Swaziland I had a dream about Khumbulile. In the dream my two grandmothers came to me. My grandmothers died before I had a chance to know them and I have no photographs of them. In the dream I knew without a doubt that these two women were my grandmothers. They were trying to speak to me. I kept trying to get a better look at them. I could see them out of my peripheral vision but as soon as I looked at them straight on, the images blurred or faded. I was distracted and turned my head back and forth experimenting with how I might see them better when my maternal grandmother became impaÑtient and said, 'It's not important whether you can see us or not. Listen to me.'

She immediately had my attention. I stopped moving. She said, 'You must give Khumbulile your royal blue blazer.' I thought it was a nice idea, to give Khumbulile something that I wore, something to remember me by, but not that jacket. It was my favourite. I loved the colour and it was washable. In Africa, that meant a lot to me. I was going over these thoughts in my head but I had not actually said anything yet. Next I felt, rather than heard, my grandmother's disappointment in me. She said, 'Not only must you give her your blue blazer, but now you must give her your turquoise velour top.' I was stunned. That top had become very special to me. The colour was soothing and it seemed to help me in some subtle way I couldn't explain. I knew my grandmothers had about had it with me. I had not responded immediately to their first request and now I had to give up something else I loved. In the dream I said, 'Okay, okay, I'll do it.'

The healers had told me that their lives improved the day they were able to stop questioning the requests of their ancestors and simply carry out the task at hand. I remember thinking this is what they had meant. I am not sure which grandmother spoke next. Her message was stern but warmer and loving. She said, 'You not only have to give Khumbulile your blazer and your shirt, but also one of Granny Baker's hangers.' My husband's grandmother had crocheted some hangers for us that I have travelled around with for years. I had given some away over the years and now only had a few I used every day. I had gotten attached to them. I said I would give the hanger away and was prepared to do whatever they were going to ask me to do. I wasn't happy about it but I had surrendered. That was the end of the dream.

The next day I woke up feeling great. I went immediately to my closet and got out the blazer, the shirt and the hanger and put them in a bag. I was scheduled for one last visit to say goodbye to Khumbulile that day. I gave her the things and told her about the dream. She thanked my grandmothers, not me! She tried on the blazer and was pleased. She admired the other things then placed them next to her so we could continue our visit. I wanted her to thank me for the gifts, so I told her exactly how much these things meant to me. She smiled and said, 'Yes, I am grateful to your ancestors. You brought them to me but it was your grandmothers who are giving me the gifts.' I laughed and shook my head. She and I both knew what my lesson was. Like the other healers, Khumbulile could always make a point or help me through a hard lesson with laughter and simple, direct language.

PH Mntshali told me once that the most important thing we can do is to listen to our ancestors, pay attention to our intuition. It wasn't necessary to like or even understand what we were being asked to do. Obeying the instruction was the key. He said that sometimes it eventually becomes evident why we were asked to do a certain thing, but not always. A person can reach a point in their lives, like the healers, where understanding is no longer even important. PH said that I could be very hard on myself. He saw this in other westerners as well. In relaying my dream to him I said I was disappointed in myself for not taking the first instruction from the grandmothers immediately. PH was amused and reminded me of the following story.

In early December 1993, I had to cancel an appointment with PH. I sent a letter and got word back that it was fine to reschedule after the new year. On 3 December 1994, the evening before my original appointment, I learned that I would be free the next day. I felt a strong urge to visit PH, but there was no way I could reach him. I decided to go see him anyway, since the thought to visit was so strong. I drove the two hours in intense summer sun. I was sticking to the seat of my Land-Rover even with the air conditioner on. PH's wife greeted me at the homestead and told me he had gone into Mbabane to sort out a government pension check he had received. We had probably passed each other on the road. PH was on a crowded bus for a two-hour ride with no air conditioning. PH's wife said I should either wait or come back in two hours. I pointed out that it would take much longer than that for PH to resolve his business and find a bus to bring him back, not to mention the long walk back to his home from the main road.

Mrs Mntshali was adamant: I must come back. She was sure PH would be returning to see me. Even though my intuition was strong and I knew she was correct, that logical part of my brain wasn't buying it. I said goodbye and was doubtful about returning that afternoon. I headed into Manzini, a little more than an hour's drive back in the direction of my home. I stopped for lunch in a little Italian restaurant. Good restaurants are few and far between so this was a great experience. I relaxed and enjoyed myself. After lunch I began having the thought, 'Wouldn't it be fun to drive back and see PH.' This was absurd: to drive back in that heat would be anything but fun. In the end something made me get into the truck and head back to PH's.

When I arrived PH's wife came out to greet me. I felt PH was near. As his wife walked toward me, PH came out of one of the huts. He stopped when he saw me, shook his head, gave me a smile and said, 'I should have known it would be you.' He had left early in the morning and had an unpleasant journey into Mbabane. On reaching the government office he was told the person he needed to see was out but would be back after lunch. Though he had decided to stay and wait for this office worker, he began having the thought that he should go home. He still had business to do, plus the ride home at midday would be awful, but the thought kept coming. He decided he would do as he was being told and get on the bus. The ride was hot, crowded and smelly. All the way home he was cursing having to follow these instructions his ancestors gave him. He was cursing but he didn't resist. PH said it would be wonderful to remain calm and follow our intuition with ease, to never feel resentment or discomfort, but we are human. If we follow our intuition, our instructions from our ancestors, we are happier. What we are to do in our day-to-day life is much clearer. We sense a general direction but do not have to be obsessed with the details.

PH threw bones for me for the first time that day and identified the ancestors who influence me most. He told me of my maternal grandfather, who died when I was four years old. I have only one memory of him, but have felt unusually close to him over my lifetime. The other ancestor, my father, died suddenly when I was thirteen years old. I was told that not only was I lucky that these powerful ancestors were watching over me but they were also in alignment with my husband's ancestors and offered him protection as well. PH told me many stories about my father and grandfather's lives. There were many stories of how these men had intervened in my own life, told with impressive detail.

I called my mother in the United States and told her some of the stories. She was pleased and seemed to enjoy hearing about her favourite men. It struck me that my mother and I had never spoken about the healers' throwing bones, neither the technique nor how they were able to access information that would not have been available to them in any ordinary way. Yet the conversation we were having felt as if we'd spoken about this phenomenon hundreds of times. Then I told my mother that PH had seen my grandfather around cattle as a young man. She said that was wrong and reminded me that her father was a city person and spent most of his life in Milwaukee, Wisconsin. She immediately changed the subject to discuss how my brother's and sister's families were, how her job was, everyday sorts of things. At the end of our conversation she said, 'Wait a minute, I just remembered my father began courting my mother while she was still at home. Her parents lived on a dairy farm, with many cows, in the countryside.'

I rarely gave the healers information about my family. At first it was the sceptic in me. Later it was unnecessary. I remember an interview with Khumbulile which she interrupted to mention that my mother was having trouble with her right hip. I said no, that in fact she was walking regularly, had taken up golf at age 70 and was in good health. That afternoon I received an airmail letter from my mother which began, 'Everything is fine here except for this annoying soreness in my right hip.' As dramatic as some of my experiences were, I was less interested in gathering evidence of the healers' abilities than I was drawn to the simple principles by which they led their lives.

I was encouraged by PH to perform a ceremony for each of my main ancestors or guides. He read my thoughts when he said, 'You may be uncomfortable with this idea. Europeans often find this awkward. Let me tell you how to go about it. You need to remember your ancestors. Start with the grandfather. What was his name? Where did he grow up? What was he like as a grown man? What memories can your mother share with you about her father? Collect stories, memories to honour. Bring out any mementoes of your grandfather, a photograph, any small thing you might have of his. Then find out what his favourite foods were and prepare them at a special time that is to be for his memory only. You may invite many or no guests. It depends on how you are feeling about it. You must wear a white cloth over your clothing for the ceremony. It will strengthen your contact with this ancestor during the feast.'

I was worried. I have only one small snapshot of my grandfather and two of my father. I have nothing that belonged to either of them. PH said this didn't matter. Their protection of me and my family was strong. I could even do the ceremony without photographs or physical objects. Just before serving the meal, I was to place a small amount of each dish served on the floor for the ancestors. This was to acknowledge that the ancestors no longer use a body. The nourishment we offer them from the physical world is merely symbolic. I was to tell stories about my grandfather and remember him as best I could while I was preparing the meal and during the meal itself. I was to share these stories with those that attended.

I talked to my mother, culled a few good stories and decided on what food I would prepare. The evening came for the ceremony. I decided I would have this first experience with only my husband and son. I chose a white bed sheet to wear toga-style over my clothes. I felt silly putting it on but my son loved it. Joseph ran to put on his favourite Teenage Mutant Ninja Turtles sheet. He was excited and wanted to hear any and all stories about his great grandfather. It was starting to be fun, though I could see Ron was uncomfortable. At the last minute, however, he ran downstairs and came back up with a blue sheet wrapped around him. We all laughed. The tension broken, we sat down to an evening of my grandfather's favourite foods and stories.

I noticed a great lifting of pressure, a physical relief for several days after the ceremony. My dreams, including those about my grandfather, increased and became more explicit in detail. I couldn't say that it was directly related to having done the ceremony to honour my grandfather, but on the other hand, it certainly didn't hurt. Shortly after that I decided to do a ceremony for my father. My father suffered from ulcers but loved hot spicy food. I prepared a Mexican meal. This time I had more memories popping up throughout the preparation and eating of the meal. Ron and Joseph were lighthearted and joked about the stories I told. It was good irreverent fun.

PH was pleased that I had done the ceremonies and said my dreams would now improve in quality. I could promote interaction with my ancestors during dreams by wearing white when I slept. I decided to try that bit of advice too. Sure enough, even today, on the evenings I wear white to bed, my dreams are indeed clear and easy to remember.

Prior to my first healer interview, I prepared a strategic plan on my computer, complete with deadlines and deliverables. I never used the plan. I found the process with the healers to be very intuitive, starting with my interview format. My first interview with a healer was Ñimminent and I wondered just what I was going to ask. I was impressed with the incredible opportunity the healers were giving me but also realised that if I was inadvertently insensitive to their culture in my first interviews, the project would be over. I conferred with many people in the medical community during this time, as well as other professionals interested in my access to the healers. I tried to draft interview questions, but even with this help, nothing came.

The day before my first interview I still had nothing. This was unnerving. Late that afternoon I was outside on our veranda talking to my son and his playmates when I felt an impulse to sit at my computer. I ran down to my office in the house and began typing out questions. Far from being scientific, this was a stream of questions coming fast, one right after the other. I ended up at a dead halt after two pages. There was nothing more. I had my interview format.

I remember thinking I should prepare an outline of chapters for my book but nothing came to mind. Several months later I was in my house again and had an actual picture come into my mind of a paper with the chapters on it. I went immediately to my office and typed out the chapters. During my next interview with Mrs Dube, senior healer, I asked my interpreter to go over the chapter outline. I probed throughout to be sure she understood. Finally we had finished and all was quiet in the room. I tensed. What if I had gotten this all wrong? Mrs Dube folded her hands and looked at me. She said I was a close friend of the healers. She said she could not improve on nor would she change anything I had written. She said my intuition or instructions from my ancestors was coming across very clearly. She was pleased.

Today I have a much greater belief that we all have ancestral spirits who guide and protect us. It is possible to feel their presence to varying degrees and receive their messages through intuition and what I like to think of as 'happy coincidences'. One such example arose when I was to drive to Manzini, a bustling little commercial centre about thirty miles south of Mbabane, to collect my interpreter. We were to proceed south to interview a healer. Three different times I headed east. I was with my friend and photographer, Albert, who found the whole thing comical, and pointed out each time that I was going the wrong way.

I noticed that Nomvula, my interpreter, never said a word, just let things run their course. She was so calm, unhurried. I was frustrated. Nomvula said, 'Can you feel it? You are being delayed. You only go so far, then turn around and head back each time. If your ancestors wanted to change your path for some protective reason, you would not 'remember' to turn around. You would keep going and end up at a different destination than the one you had planned.'

I relaxed and we carried on to our destination, where I learned that during our 'delay', the healer I was to interview was called away unexpectedly. This allowed me to meet his wife, a gifted trainer of healers. It was crystal clear when she walked out of their house that she was the reason I was there. I couldn't explain why, but I was so happy to see her, though we'd never met. She greeted us with such joy and was prepared to be interviewed as if that was what we had planned. We chatted and visited all afternoon like long-lost sisters.

Spending time with the healers always had the same quality for me. The visit was always very pleasant. Pleasant is probably an understatement. I felt as if I knew the person, though we may have been meeting for the first time. Time seemed to take on an illusory quality. I could walk out of a visit or an interview thinking it had lasted thirty minutes, look at my watch and realise we had been talking for five hours. The reverse could also happen. I would guess we had been together for two hours when in fact it had been half an hour.

The healers believe that time is only relative to our physical existence. They explained that when they speak with the ancestors and interact through visions that there is no time. It is as if all things happen simultaneously. We are born, we are alive, we die, we are spirits, it is all happening at the same time. When a sangoma is throwing bones and appears to be predicting the future, she is actually discussing events that are happening now. I was taken by surprise when one of the healers told me I had a teenage daughter. I remember thinking: 'Aha! I've caught her.

She's wrong,' but before I had a chance to challenge her, she explained that my daughter was actually the spirit of a baby I had miscarried in the South Pacific. I had never mentioned that I had lived there. I certainly never discussed a miscarriage. Had that child lived she would indeed have been a teenager. In the case of a miscarriage, the healers believe the child will stay with and be raised by the mother. Since there is no time and space in the spirit world, I had been mothering this child all along and would meet her at my death.

This was one of hundreds of healing moments the healers gave me. An experience that had left vestiges of unresolved grief was brought full circle. At the time the healer told me about my daughter, I saw the child for a moment. She was distant in my peripheral vision, yet I had a strong feel for her personality. I could see she was tall, slender, with long light brown hair. It felt very natural. It was like being with my son after not having seen him for a couple of hours. She was very familiar, as if she lived with me. I could see her smiling. It was very comforting.

I had so much to learn from these healers.

2

Our spirit guides – the ancestors

he healers describe the 'ancestors' as spirits, much like guardian angels. I enjoyed their stories, but thought of the 'ancestors' as just a colourful aspect of the culture, until I experienced explicit dreams myself. My deceased maternal grandfather, both grandmothers and my father began giving me direct instructions. As the healers had said, it was not frightening in any way.

As in my experience, the ancestors may make contact through a healer's consultation or through personal dreams, but it is not always so clear why they ask us to do certain things. For instance, a healer in Nelspruit, South Africa, was told in a dream that she should visit her grandmother's grave, where there would be a white goat for her. The grave was quite a distance from her homestead but nevertheless she journeyed to this place the next day. Arriving at the grave, she saw a white goat. She called the goat by her grandmother's name, and it came to her, like a pet. Now, in southern Africa, a goat is for eating, not a domestic animal. Nevertheless, the sangoma decided to bring the goat home. It became her pet, only answering to the name of the grandmother. To her surprise, the community treated it with love and respect. The animal is protected and to this day, clearly enjoys its new-found home.

The healer did not and may never know why the goat was to live with her. The reason may not be revealed to her in this lifetime, but that is not important. The healers all tell stories of the ancestors asking them to do unusual things. Initially, they resist or delay in carrying out the action, only to find their lives becoming uncomfortable in some way. Finally, upon carrying out the wishes of the ancestors, they are well and happy again. Often the action results in a direct benefit to the healer. After enough of these experiences, the healers seem to enter a state of trust in which anything from the mere hint of an intuition to a clear and vividly detailed direction from the ancestors is acted upon. They no longer ask why.

Khumbulile Mdluli, a Swazi healer, explains: 'When a thought comes to my mind, and keeps coming back, I know it is guidance from my ancestors. My ancestors told me where to build my clinic and how it should look. I have always followed my ancestors correctly and exactly, ever since training. With modernisation and change in lifestyle, people begin to see this contact with their ancestors as something primitive. They ignore the attempts of the ancestors to make contact. A person is in the wrong job, the ancestors do not want him in that job. But he ignores a thought such as "I must go and work for Mrs Smith" because it does not make sense. This may be an important gift to him. He must show the ancestors that he is willing. He can do a simple thing first, like finding out what type of work Mrs Smith does. Perhaps he will then write or go and meet her. There are more culprits in the world today because we are losing touch with our own cultures, losing this help from ancestors. We are losing our ability to make spiritual contact.'

P H Mntshali, a Zulu healer, elaborates: 'I would say throw away the idea that people die. Also, people who are killed turn out to be helpful because they forgive, they come out with a certain empathy and sympathy. They do good and powerful work. Because they did not do their work assignment in their own lives, they have work to do now. It may not look as we expect it to, this sympathising. For instance, a child might be possessed or chosen. The ancestor wants that child to be out of school, to stop their formal education. You ask: "How can that be good? How can that be sympathising with the child?" But I say, "What is schooling? Is this education?" This European education, it is only a small view.

'You cannot weigh your own life. The ancestors come to give you a legacy, they know what is the best life for you. They are serving you. You may think you know better but you cannot have all the information, only the ancestors can see the whole picture. The ancestors will take younger people, either possess them earlier or bring them to the next life sooner. The ancestors see how a person's life may go. They come early and prevent the person from going on a harmful or less satisfying path. Unusual and sudden death of young people, car accidents and such, are the ancestors taking that child at the moment they must, in order to protect their spiritual growth.

'The ancestors are aware when you do not like them or their way. They work on their own schedule, their own time. They will have tried three or four times to reach your family, perhaps through your father, your mother, then your brother, but have failed. They see you and say, "Okay, now is the time". They decide to take you. They are fed up, the time is now, they don't care about education, travel plans, marriage. The time is now and you must carry out the legacy of your family. It is sort of in frustration that the ancestors may go after the younger ones. But when these young ones grow older they always, without exception, will see it was a gift to be a healer. They often show exceptional talent and compassion. They practise very late into their lives and are happy. These ones that are possessed young, they are special to us all.

'This idea of legacy works the same for healers and non-healers alike. Suppose your family has a legacy to create great and beautiful music. Perhaps this legacy comes first to your grandmother. She begins to follow her calling, but works hard on a farm, has many children. The husband and family do not support her passion. She gives up her talent but always feels there is something missing. Some part of her heart aches until she passes on to the next life. Next the ancestors try your father. He has always been drawn to music. He goes even further with his talent but his faith falters when his income is not steady and reliable. He has mouths to feed, children to put through school, medical bills to pay. He abandons his mission, plays a bit of music at home for the family, but remains restless.

'The ancestors may become frustrated now. No one yet has the strength to follow through on this magnificent gift. A generation is skipped. You begin to notice that your small daughter loves to be near her grandfather when he picks up a musical instrument. She is drawn to him. After the grandfather dies, the ancestors make contact with the child. She becomes possessed of the talent. She has the gift. You remember your father's dreams of developing his own musical gift and you encourage your daughter's interest. One thing leads to another, the child becomes a woman. Through the beauty of her music she makes her own contribution to healing. It is not always an easy or steady life for her but she has accepted her calling. Her gift grows and she shares it late into her old age. Now the ancestors are pleased. A legacy, a thing of beauty and healing has been passed on.

'We all know when we are not following our calling. We are unhappy. It is as simple as that. We are restless. We do not like the people we work with. We do not like our work. We must move on. This work, these people, it is not their fault. We are in the wrong place. It is so important to take responsibility for our own healing, for our own lives. We thank God and the ancestors for giving us that work. It taught us some lessons that we will surely use as we seek out our true calling. We honour our ancestors, we pray for clearer guidance. It will be shown to us at the right time.

'As for financial security, it all depends on how you obey orders. If you obey exactly as the ancestors direct, your practice, your life, will not fail. The ancestors will provide. They will show you a way. At first you may worry. How will you pay your bills, the children's' school fees? Then you become so caught up in your calling, your true work, your love for it grows. Soon you are only serving and not worrying so much about the bills. When you need it most, money or goods arrive. Your calling is God's work. God does not call us then leave us to drown in hardship.

'So this is my belief – that people do not actually die, they pass over, then contact us. They help us. We learn that we are on this earth by the will of God. The ancestors use us as instruments to do their work. In the old days, people were easily in contact with their ancestors. They honoured and were able to contact the ancestors easily. Their close contact with the ancestors healed physical ailments and personal relationships. I am talking here about the average person, not necessarily healers. All people knew how to honour and contact their ancestors. They were guided and well protected. Today there is a loss of respect and understanding of the traditional ways in this regard.

'Your special angel who looks after you feels great shame when you are not listening. You decide, with your limited human knowledge, not to consult your ancestors. In the old days, people explored and travelled far, but always looked to the ancestors for a clearance, a sign that they were on the right track. The ancestors used to come closer and give a clearance straight away. You would have a dream or a feeling straight away. Ancestors are assigned to look after you. They stay and work for you until you succeed, until you meet and fulfil your desires, which are God's will for you.

'When you have a feeling not to go somewhere, to do or not do something, this is direct guidance that we must respect. Human life is always guided, it is balanced by your angel, your ancestor. People now are so learned, so wilful. They forget that they go with somebody, this guide that they must obey. I see spoiled people who have lost touch. They say they live by God but their actions show otherwise. God is the big boss but he cannot work with everyone, so God works with ancestors, your ancestors, my ancestors.

'We all go on to become ancestors at some point in time. For example, you are a mother. Are you going to forget your children when you pass away? No, you will be their ancestor and help them, give them instructions. You now have a better focus. You have a better understanding of that world you were just in, what is good, what is wrong. When your children die, who do you expect them to report to first? You say, "Come see your mother, straight away." Of course! This is exactly as it should be. This is the proper order of things. You will ask them, "How did you get here?" "Oh Mom, it was a car accident." You will answer, "Honestly, I told you long ago to drive carefully." You will laugh together. They are your progeny, they cannot be accepted without going to you first. You will guide and welcome them into this new world with much love.'

Mrs Ntombemhlophe Dube tells us about an ancestor who came to help her with her healing. 'This ancestor', Mrs Dube begins, 'is from Mozambique. He was killed by my great grandfather, the Swazi warrior. This ancestor from Mozambique came to me two years after I had finished my training. The first time he came, I was attending the graduation ceremony of one of my friends. When the drums were being beaten to welcome the new traditional healers, this ancestor just rose up in me. It was not even at night. He introduced himself to me. He explained who he was, how he came to be my ancestor. I could only hear and understand his words. After he had come several more times, I began to see him. He was a very big man. He carried the tail of a buck, it was black and white. He helped with patients during the day. One of his specialities is to dispel bad medicines patients have been given before coming to me. This ancestor is a great help to me even today.

'My two main ancestors have not changed in appearance in all these years because they were fully grown men when they died. Recently I have been possessed by a new ancestor, a boy child who is thirteen years old. This is surprising after so many years of working only with these two ancestors, now a new friend arrives. I notice that he influences me to choose younger looking clothing. When I am drawn to this clothing, it means he will be making contact with me soon. My forefathers killed this boy. They wanted some meat, so they killed this boy looking after the cattle. When he is around, I often feel like being near cattle or even driving some cattle out to pasture or playing with some younger children. At times I see a vision of a young boy in front of me. He is playful and I enjoy his presence. He will be of help to me but for now, we are just taking our time getting used to each other.

'The ancestors are wise and gentle spirits. They come for purposes of healing patients, but they also guide us in our day-to-day life. This house we are sitting in, the ancestors told me in a dream that I must build a house, exactly like this, exactly in this spot. The ancestors showed me exactly what it looked like. By building it, I honoured my ancestors. I followed their instructions. Behind us is a house with no roof. I have been advised by my ancestors to remove that roof, remove the thatch. They say the roof must be replaced with smaller tiles or, maybe aluminium roofing. I do not have the money to put up new roofing. I don't know how I will get the money. It is a hardship now, but the end result will improve my life and my practice. I know. I have seen this before.

'If a person dies they might not become an ancestor immediately. They may need more time until they are ready to become an ancestor. If I died right now, I don't think I would immediately possess another person. I will stay for several generations until I am ready to possess and guide, be an ancestor. When a healer dies, if there is no one to carry on the tradition of healing in the family, the family will keep and continue to pass on, generation to generation, the items and articles the original healer used in their practice. Some day, even many generations later, someone will be possessed and use those exact same items again.

'Healers are not frightened by death. We have contact with people who have died. Death is comfortable to us and we are able to help people who are facing death. We can calm their fears and help them make a more peaceful transition. The ancestors do not want the loved ones left behind to mourn a lot, because the person who has died feels this. It is a weight on them. It prevents the passage from happening smoothly and quickly. It is best to be happy for the new life the dead person is enjoying. We all have a certain time when we will be called, when we must die. On this day you can be anywhere, even where there is tight security. When the hour and the time come you must pass on. There is nothing that can prevent this. It is as it should be.'

'Our ancestors are so clever and loving. They can really make us laugh at ourselves,' says Nhlavana Maseko, President of the Traditional Healers Organisation for Africa (THO), 'like the time PH Mntshali was a young man. So well-known a healer today, but I knew him before he was possessed. He was learning things about herbs in his dreams and developing a respect for what the herbal treatments could do. But he did not want to become a healer. He came to see me as a patient once when he was not feeling well. He was still working with the government of Swaziland and driving a car in those early days. I diagnosed him. I told him he would become a possessed healer. But he said, "No, I am not going to be a healer!" He was so strong about this, until one day while driving, his car spoke to him. The ancestors knew how much PH loved his car. They could get his attention through this thing he so admired. At last he agreed, but it was not easy for him. He really resisted. You see how PH loves his work being a healer. He helps so many people. It is hard to imagine, forty-odd years ago, that he was a tough case for the ancestors.'

The first ancestor to come to Mrs Sibandze of Matsapha was her paternal grandmother. Kunene was her name. Mrs Sibandze tells the story: 'Kunene never completed her healer training and was never really successful in her life because of this. The ancestors passed this healing gift through the family to me. I was born in 1942 but Kunene did not come to me until 1966. In a dream she actually showed me the name of the healer who was to train me. I went to KwaZulu-Natal in South Africa for training. Today Kunene is still helping me with treatments, and telling me when and from where my patients will come. She is pleased I am finishing her work.

'The ancestors are like good friends. You just love them so much. They help not only with my health practice but even with my family and on many other issues. They can come at any time, night or day. In the past, everybody was in touch with their ancestors. Things changed in Africa when the missionaries arrived. They may have come with the proper intentions and good hearts but they didn't understand our spiritual life was already strong. In the missionary primary schools we were taught that ancestors were part and parcel with snakes and so on, they were an evil thing. People began to fall away from the ancestors. I believe there are some people who have good conduct by themselves, without going to any organised church. I believe those people are being well guided by their ancestors and God. They do not necessarily need the guidance or structure of a organised church. Churches do play a part for the others though. They can teach about love, respect and kindness. The general principles are good and pure. The many man-made rules are what get in the way.

'There is a siSwati word for angel, a helper spirit, but it also means good ancestors. In Xhosa, there is another word which means angel. I believe the ancestors are angels who guide us to become better people. They help us make our contribution, in this lifetime. When a person is ready to die, the ancestors will come and let the family know. A healer can help the dying person's ancestors come out a last time and give the person's instructions, what should be done after their death. It is a beautiful thing. You see, the ancestors are helping us. They are at our sides, always.'

'I have eight ancestors,' begins Nomsa Vilakati. 'The first one to come was the great grandmother, on my mother's side. She came in a vision during the day. I was looking after cattle as a young girl, but I began to play around. The cattle started to graze on someone else's land, on some planted maize. I was afraid I would be punished. I found a place to hide and was kneeling down under a bush. Then a buck, an impala, came right up to my back and touched me with its forelegs. I turned around thinking that it was a person who had come to punish me. I was shocked to see this buck, a wild animal that could harm me. Without thinking I grabbed its head, twisted it and killed it. I was very excited and went home to report this to the elders. They did not pay it much attention. They were not sure what I meant by this story. That same night a dream came to me. It was this same grandmother. She told me to take the leather, the skin of the impala I killed and wear it.

'I reported killing the impala to my father. He thought I was talking about a goat. My father went to the scene and saw it was a buck. It was impossible that a small girl could kill such a buck. An impala is dangerous and can even kill a man. It is nearly impossible to kill it with one's hands. My father wondered how this could have happened. He could not get it out of his mind. It made no sense to him. He went to a traditional healer that he knew and asked what was going on with his daughter, Nomsa. The healer said, "That impala was killed a long time ago by the same grandmother who has spoken to Nomsa through visions. The grandmother sent that impala to Nomsa so she could wear the skin. It is especially for her. She is a young girl and while watching the cattle, she feels free and even forgets at times to wear a skin or clothing. But now when she is watching the cattle, she will notice a feeling of worry or panic. She will find herself thinking about this particular impala skin and she will wear it. Immediately after putting it on, she will feel very good and much relieved. This is her ancestor's way of telling her to put the skin on."

'My father did not tell me these things, yet they happened just as the healer said. That skin was my friend. Time passed and I began to grow up. I even fell in love with a young man. When I tried to go off and meet this young man somewhere, the ancestor would come and stop me. She would say, "Once you go with this man, then you and I will become separated." I could not be separated from this grandmother I loved so much.

'This ancestor and others are always guiding me. They helped me to build this home. During my sleep I was shown who was the chief to approach for land. I was told that money would come to me. I was afraid to approach the chief because I had no reason to think he would give me any land, but I did go to him as the ancestors said. At first I was unsure and embarrassed; who was I to be asking for this big favour, to be given land. Just as I was preparing to excuse myself he said he had a parcel of land for me. I couldn't believe my good fortune. This was before I was a healer, even then the ancestors were helping me, picking the ground, showing me the way to pay for it. When I die, those ancestors will go on to possess other members of my family. This healing legacy will carry on.'

Khumbulile Mdluli, a Swazi healer, once told me that her ancestors wished me to be alert for 'a European woman' I would meet. I would know her by the name of Margaret, with a last name starting with 'W'. The ancestors wanted me to give Margaret some information about Khumbulile. I would know when and what type of information to pass on. Margaret would be of help to both me and Khumbulile.

It wasn't clear where I would meet Margaret and whether she was simply of European heritage or actually lived in Europe today. In late 1994 I moved to Washington, DC and forgot about Margaret. Over the next several months I transcribed my African interviews and prepared for an assignment in Warsaw. One month before I left Washington for Poland, I had an early morning dream. My maternal grandmother asked me to: 'Wake up and work on the interviews, now. It must be ready for her.' I did as she asked, finished the work and packed for my move to Poland. Then a former colleague of mine from Botswana rang. He had heard I was spending some time with indigenous healers, would I like to meet a Polish healer? David gave me the name of a Mietek Wirkus, a Polish émigré to the USA. Mietek manages a research foundation, teaches healers and maintains his own healing practice. His clients include many highly placed officials and scientists. I was surprised he had time to see me.

The day of my appointment started out oddly. I drove to Mietek's office in the Washington suburb of Bethesda. The office is in the centre of a busy commercial district and I was lucky to find a parking spot. I locked my doors and checked all was secure in the car. I walked across the street to the appointment and thoroughly enjoyed meeting Mietek Wirkus, healer extraordinary. He told me that his wife would come to Warsaw and introduce me to a healer friend of theirs. His wife happened to be in town and I could meet her now. Margaret Wirkus was a delight and we chatted at length. Finally, I returned to my car and found the motor on, the keys in the ignition and the door unlocked. I was shocked that the car was still there, given the circumstances, and dumbfounded that I had no memory of leaving such an open invitation to car thieves.

Early the next morning I had another dream. In this dream Khumbulile Mdluli was sitting in her traditional clinic in Swaziland and trying to speak to me. Her mouth moved but I couldn't make out any words. I was so happy to see her, such a nice reprieve from the bustle of Washington, that I wasn't really paying attention to what she was trying to communicate. Exasperated with me, Khumbulile grabbed a piece of paper off the floor near where she sat and wrote M-A-R-G-..., and suddenly it came back to me. I yelled: 'Margaret Wirkus?' Khumbulile nodded her head yes, and smiled. The dream ended. I shot out of bed, frantically looking for something with information about Khumbulile on it. All my things were packed and only a draft manuscript with my African interviews mentioned her work. I put a copy of the manuscript into an envelope and had it couriered across town to Margaret.

Margaret was leaving for Italy to lecture, but read the document on the airplane. She rang me on her return and thus began a long relationship that shaped my experience and work with the indigenous healers in Poland, and continues on international issues today. Margaret and Khumbulile corresponded and finally met in the USA in June 1997 when Khumbulile, sponsored by the Wirkus Foundation, addressed an international conference of indigenous healers and medical professionals.

3

Passing on the gift – the trainers speak

The training period for traditional healers can last from one to ten years, during which time the students may not see their spouses or children, must abstain from sexual contact and often live under harsh conditions. All this is part of a cleansing process to prepare the healer for his or her life's work, and the experiences of training earn a deep place in their memories. The healers shared with me some of their trials in finding and enduring this training.

Mrs Ntombemhlophe Dube told me: 'I was in training at Bhunya with Mrs Vilakati for three years. I left my husband alone with our two-year-old child. The other children stayed with relatives. It is a rule of the training that you cannot see your family. I was told this on the first day I entered training. I missed my husband and my children. This emotional pain was the most difficult. Before I finished the training, I began to feel comfortable with the healers and their ways. Learning the plants and the herbs was very interesting because of the way it happened. My ancestor was very active and would come to me in dreams, show me the different herbs and plants. Because of this, I began to enjoy learning about herbs and plants. The other healers and trainees began to feel like my family. It was only difficult when a visiting healer might come with her or his children.

'In training it is not always the trainer who teaches you a speciality, rather the ancestors visit you in the night and give you your speciality. They teach you what you need to know about that disease. You may acquire a speciality that your trainer is not knowledgeable about. My most memorable experience during training was throwing the bones. It came quite easily and I loved it. Now I do not enjoy it as much. I have high blood pressure. When throwing bones your mind and spirit are quite active, you have to talk a lot, it is stressful. This is hard on my blood pressure.

'I finished my training, graduated and returned home. At that time only one patient visited me. So I threw bones and told that patient every little thing that was wrong with him. The patient was quite impressed and told other people about Mrs Dube, the new healer. This is how it starts. Our practice grows slowly, giving us time to gain confidence, to feel more relaxed with our ability and our relationship with our ancestors. After some time, we have many patients; the word of our expertise and specialities spreads. We are busy and happy doing the ancestors' work.

'Early in my practice, I met a man who was suffering from an incurable wound. I had no training or experience with incurable wounds such as this. This sick man had already visited many, many healers and doctors. I did not want him coming to me. If I failed, everyone would doubt my ability as a healer. I was nervous. The wound was on top of his foot. Flesh was growing on the wound. The doctors had to cut this flesh off for him because it was growing so rapidly.

'I asked why he had come to see me, since I know nothing about this type of disease. The patient said, "I was told that you can help me." I decided this patient should leave my clinic because I could not help him, but just as I was getting ready to chase him away the ancestors came and told me to stop. Instead of chasing him away, I must accommodate him. During the night the ancestors came and told me how to cure this disease. The ancestor showed me the right herbs and many alternatives for healing the man. The following morning I went immediately to the bush to find the herbs the ancestors told me about in my dreams. I went without even greeting the patient. Then I prepared the herbs as my ancestors showed me, cleaned the man's wound and applied the herbs as I was shown. I gave the man herbs to take home with him. I told him he must remove the treatment, clean the wound and apply again every three days.

'The patient returned home. After three weeks he came back to see me. The flesh on the wound had fallen off on its own and it was finally healing. I noticed that now a deep small hole had developed on his foot. I applied the same herbs and gave some to the man to apply at home and that hole was healed. I was very impressed because I never thought I could treat such a wound. The doctors had told the patient that if the wound did not heal they would amputate the whole leg. The patient was so relieved that he did not pay the usual amount but paid me an entire herd of cattle.

'This did not become a speciality for me. It is like that sometimes. The ancestors have a special type of wound they want you to treat for a particular person. It is up to our ancestors what we do with the new knowÑledge. Sometimes it has a limited purpose.

'One of my ancestors is my grandfather; another is a Mozambique man with two sons. I have two different types of ancestors, therefore I must have two different houses for these two families. I do have two houses for them at my clinic. If I am being possessed by my grandfather, I have one type of attire. If it is the Mozambican, he has his own different clothing. Every ancestor has a different name. When they come to possess me, they greet me so I know them. I know what attire I must put on. Or I may find I am attracted to certain types of clothing. I find that if I wear a certain attire, it makes me feel happy; I realise one of my ancestors is coming to me. When you have been possessed by an ancestor, it is as if you are unconscious. You do not feel that it is happening. If the ancestor is very powerful, then you yourself will feel very powerful, it will be a strong experience. If the ancestor is not so strong, it will be a softer experience, a softer but good, not frightening experience.'

Nhlavana Maseko told me: 'Spiritually, you are very healthy during training. At times, especially when foreign spirits come for weeks at a time, that can be difficult. I would not eat for up to twenty days, drinking only herbal concoctions. My limbs would hurt or ache but I would feel very well spiritually. Even now I can drink only herbal concoctions for days at a time and feel strong. My body feels clean. It is good. I feel healthy.

'Foreign spirits are not of your family. That is all it means. Foreign spirits are not your ancestors. My forefathers, for instance, were warriors and they killed some people. When these people were killed, they became my family's foreign spirits. There must be a working relationship with your foreign spirit and your ancestors. They have something, an injustice, a murder that must be worked out, must be healed. This is what is happening when you feel spiritually well, but your body is aching. Your ancestors and the foreign spirits are working out their relationship. They must combine; it is not an easy thing.

'During training, as the ancestors come out, you have to finish up with your own ancestors first. That relationship sorts itself out, then you are ready to work with the foreign spirits. It happens in a natural way. The ancestors do the work through you. Maybe the foreign spirit wants to be the more important or senior ancestor; when the ancestor of your clan comes, well, they may have to fight it out. You might feel some aches during this time. It is this friction among them that is working itself out. However, if you first follow the instructions of your ancestors, they always will come first. Complete their instructions exactly as they want you to do. Then when the foreign spirits come, you talk with them and with your ancestors. It can all work out beautifully.

'A foreign spirit is someone who likes you very much and wants to come to you. Evil spirits are something completely different. I am only talking about good spirits. Good spirits give you direction, protect you, guide you. They are helpful. There are some medicines and certain types of clothing you can wear that promote this relationship between your ancestors and the foreign spirits. The foreign spirits and the ancestors combine their efforts and it becomes easy. You can undertake anything you want, and it will go smoothly. Also at home, at your traditional clinic, you can separate the spirits, have different ancestral huts for them. This is helpful.

'After training, I heard voices that said my grandfather, the great healer, had died. I had to go back and take over. I went back to my mission school to visit. You remember I ran away from home and was taken in by a Christian missionary family. This family saw my traditional attire and the ochre on my head. They said, "Oh, what is all this about?" My missionary friend and patron didn't know what to do. He didn't know if they should sit with me, yet, they brought their children to see me. Their hearts had much love in them for me, but this thing, this traditional thing was confusing. They saw I was healthy but they were worried. Would my being a traditional healer cause them harm? They had preached in church that healers were harmful. That is what they had been taught to believe; yet they were happy to see me.

'Immediately, my patron and his missionary family put me on a train to Cape Town, South Africa. There I underwent training in 1963 at Zigaine's Herbal College. This same missionary family sponsored me there. They also sponsored me to attend the African Herbal College and the Ekhanana Herb Research Institute. There were medical doctors there trying to learn from the herbs. I saw this interest from the medical side. I understood the importance of cooperation between the two systems. We could respect one another. The doctors were happy to have me there because of my own background. I was explaining what the herbs were, how to mix them, what their healing properties were. The doctors knew about herbs only by hearsay. I was able to suggest things to them. I also attended some homeopathic training in Johannesburg. That is where I learned some German treatments. Later in 1980 the King of Swaziland sent me to Germany to learn more.

'It seems my ancestors were interested in my bringing the traditional and the modern, the western, closer together. Even as a young boy, it was no accident that I ran from my uncle, the most powerful traditional healer in the region, straight smack into the hearts and home of a Christian missionary family – a family that should have been opposed to all I came to stand for. Yet, they supported me through my very introduction to a big task, bringing the medical and the traditional closer together. This was to be my main focus for the remainder of my life. We must respect one another, all sides, all cultures, all methods of true healing. We have much to do to promote this cooperation. My training is really the story of bringing both sides of healing together.'

'I used to train healers in the past, but no longer,' says Mrs Sibandze of Matsapha. 'I am concentrating on healing. My practice has grown so large, I no longer have time for both training and patients. In a case like this the ancestors decide. Both paths, to heal and to train healers, are equally important. For me, the ancestors want my patients to come first.

'Some healers hope they do not have to be trainers because it is very difficult. You must be very strict, but also very kind and loving. The trainees must not be frightened. They are possessed and this thing is all new. They are nervous. Some have been confused, frightened, even very ill for some time before they come to training. They must know that the trainer cares about them and will not harm them. They are able to follow the strict instructions because they know they are safe and loved.

'There is a training order that is followed. The ancestors guide each trainer, show them how to train and when to teach each important task. Each trainee is encouraged according to his or her talents; some may learn more or different types of healing practices than others. It all depends on the individuals, what they are ready to learn. The graduated healers can always come back to visit their trainer and they usually do. It is always a happy occasion to see how your former trainees are doing. They come with much praise for the training they had. They have now been practising traditional medicine for a while and they can see what great benefits the training has given them. Now they understand why it had to be so strict, so disciplined. They will come with new questions and tell me new things they are discovering in their practice. It is always a helpful and happy exchange for both of us.'

Jumayina Vilakati told me: 'At home, my family believed in ancestors. My father was trained as a healer. He was sick for eight years. He became so thin. He was eating just mud along the riverside, as a snake might. He was sick from the ancestors. They were about to make him a great healer. He disappeared and came back with a water python, a symbol of being a healer. He used to bite that python under the jaw. He would suck in the blood of the snake and pour some blood into a container and just mix it with herbs. Once you do that, you do not need to go for training. That is a very special way of becoming a healer, it means you have special revelations. It is above what possessed healers like myself can do. He was an extraordinary type of healer. This happens to very few individuals. The person is directed by the ancestors and must go underwater to get this python. He will look for somebody to treat him to be strong as a healer, but will find he does not need actual training. These powers from the snake allow him to know what to do.

'I have forgotten when I began to be a healer. I know it was when they were making Sandlane Border gate to South Africa by Bhunya. When I would cross at that gate, I was not required to have a passport to enter South Africa. I went to Komatipoort for my training. I am more than 62 years old now. That was more than twenty years ago. I went for training when I was a grown woman and already had ten children.

'One year after training I began training others. It all depends on the talent of the healer and the ancestors, whether they themselves will train others and how soon after they become healers they will start to train others. I have had people come to me who have had other trainers. The trainee or even the trainer will be advised by the ancestors, through dreams or thoughts, to send the trainee to Mrs Vilakati for some 'finishing touches'. Sometimes when examining the trainee, I may see that the person is not quite ready. I send the person back for further training and have her come again, much later. I have trained between eighty and one hundred healers. There are also many in South Africa who have come for my training.

'I take people of all ages for training, some young, some mature women, some older grandmothers. The youngest one I have had was 12 years old. I prefer the younger students. They do not have children, husband or other responsibilities. They can just concentrate on the training. They are bright and catch on to things quickly. The trainees stay right here at my homestead in Bhunya. They must know, what are these herbs? Where are they found? How do they collect them? Do they come from an area that is treated with insecticides? If so, the herbs are poisonous and the natural healing properties have been harmed. The herbs must be pure. The students must then know how to prepare and properly store the herbs to maintain their healing properties.

'When the trainees have graduated and are ready to go home, I give them a list of the herbs and medicines in case they forget anything, so that they have a reference. This also helps them to retain their confidence. I also prepare a package of the bones for each trainee to take home. The bones are not all the same, though they may contain certain common things like the dominoes. When a domino is facing up after throwing bones, that means everything will just go fine. If another piece is upside down it means a family member will be coming. Another piece is a symbol for police and cars. A hand or symbol of a hand, if open, may mean that money is coming to you today. Different pieces and symbols are right for different individual healers. There is a symbol for a father: if upside down it may mean he is angry; if right side up, he is resting easily, he is happy.

'Upon graduation the trainees will use those bones for a lifetime. They learn when to refer patients during their training as well. When throwing bones, they must find out when and what medical treatment is best for the patient. Bones will tell them whether the patient should be treated by traditional medicine or modern, whether they should go to hospital or to another healer, what type of specialist, and where. The trainee must be capable of knowing this from the bone throwing.

The most difficult time during training is at night, because the trainees all become possessed. They will come to me during the night, one by one. I am not getting any sleep. This is very difficult for me, but it is all part of my duty. Even my children must wake up and beat the drums for those being possessed. The children still go to school the next day. They are very tired. This is hard on them. So you see being a trainer involves your whole family. It is a commitment and sacrifice for all of you. But just when you think you can take no more, the ancestors will give you a rest between training groups, or as you get old like myself, a break from training completely. It all works out for the best.

'There are enjoyable parts to training too. It is not all difficult. There is joy in seeing your students learn. They are working so hard. They are missing their families and not having much sleep. Being chosen by the ancestors is not an easy path for them. I love the throwing of bones. Working with the students on this gives me much pleasure. The students are happy when they are throwing bones, to be so close to the ancestors. Guiding students on throwing bones requires much strength. I do not do it so much now because I am old and tire more easily.

'Those I have trained over the years have gone on to train others. On the last visit I made to South Africa, my trainees gathered together those they had trained. I saw how many generations of training had come from my own trainees. They gave me donations to give to the trainees at my home. When they complete training and start their own practices, they remember that there will be others in training after them. They send donations to help me support those trainees as I have supported them. There will always be possessed healers because the ancestors are choosing them. This work of the ancestors, it will go on and on.'

4

Throwing bones — the truth revealed

interviewed the healers for six months before I asked about the practice of bone throwing. On a couple of occasions healers offered to throw bones for me. It didn't interest me at the time, so I declined. When I finally did ask, the healers said: 'We were waiting and watching to see when you would ask.' It is a very powerful diagnostic tool and is often the first interest when the healers are contacted by westerners. The healers said it was a good sign that I did not probe them on this matter until I had a grounding in their world. I had to understand who they were, how they had become healers, and much more, before I could focus on the bone-throwing technique.

'Bones' refer to actual bones, often those of the goat used and eaten in the healers' graduation or initiation ceremony signalling the completion of training. 'Bones' may also include dominoes, coins, a symbol of a foot or an actual foot (of a rooster or monkey), sea shells, small smooth stones and any other thing the healers' ancestors may have told them to add.

humbulile explains: 'You throw the bones and the ancestors tell you exactly what to say. It is not a matter of learning, if you are possessed. Other types of healers can force matters, trying to throw bones without being possessed. They go to non-possessed healers for muti that helps them clear their thoughts. They are then able to hear their ancestors and can temporarily throw and read the bones. With a possessed healer, this is a gift, an ability we have all our lives. We do not take any special muti to help our thoughts. This all comes directly from our ancestors. I was already throwing bones and diagnosing just two weeks into my training. I could see and hear what the ancestors wanted me to say. It was very, very clear and it came easily. The ability to throw bones does not seem to increase or decrease over time. It is just something between you and your ancestors.

'The bones I use today, ten years after my training, are the same bones I started with. I have added a few things, a new bone, a stone. My ancestors told me to add these. I have few bones, even with the ones I have added. Some healers use many bones. You see that both their hands are almost overflowing with bones when they throw. The bones are a tool. You must have the right tool for the right person. Each healer must have the right kind and number of objects to hear and understand what the ancestors are saying. Often my ancestors tell me what the bones are saying before they hit the mat. I do not have to study how they have fallen because my ancestors speak so directly and immediately to me. A possessed healer does not always have to throw the bones. Suppose I become very old and my eyesight is poor. I might ask my child – or ask you, the patient – to throw the bones, then the ancestors will speak to me about what those bones say. It might be that as I grow old, the ancestors speak so directly with me I do not even throw bones. This might happen, especially if I were to lose my eyesight.

'Each bone has a certain meaning and always refers to this meaning. For instance, I have a bone that represents the mother's side of the family. It will always tell me about the patient's mother's side of the family. Another bone might always refer to children and the number of children a person is likely to have. Or a coin, it will always speak about the person's financial future. A small green stone I have always talks about a physical ailment. Our ancestors, who help us today, were throwing bones in their day, many generations ago. Then they used only bones, not other objects. This is where the name 'bones' comes from. Today we call all our objects 'bones', the coins, the dominoes, shells.

'If I leave my bones at home and I am travelling, I can come to your house and just pick up some stones nearby and throw them. The ancestors will tell me what to say even if I do not use my own bones. I always use the same small mat to throw my bones on. If I forget my mat, then I can use a small handkerchief. It just must be something of mine, something small I can throw the bones on. I can throw the bones for any loved one, even if they are not here, if you need to know how they are. You do not need to bring a photograph of them, simply put it in your heart. Your desire to know about them, your intention, must be pure, must come with kindness and true regard for their well-being. I will throw the bones and tell you everything about them. It would be the same as if they were here.

'If you are sitting with other people when you are having bones thrown, the bones may begin talking about your friend. This is because you have a relationship with this person and the ancestors may have something to say to her or him. Even though it is your consultation, the ancestors may use the opportunity to speak to the person with you. They may need to tell them something. The ancestors will say what is most important at that moment for you to hear.

'Not all healers use bones to speak with the ancestors. Sometimes the ancestors want to speak through me, in their own voices. The ancestors decide, will they speak to us through the bones or possess us and use our bodies to speak directly to the patient? Because I have English-speaking ancestors they often speak to me in English. Healers may speak in the native tongue of the ancestor when they are possessed. Yet the healer cannot speak that language in their everyday life. Usually when a possessed healer is throwing bones the ancestors will speak to her in her own language.

'When the ancestors speak to us, it is a miracle. It is like a dream. While the patient is sitting with you, you begin to see pictures in your mind. The ancestors use thoughts and pictures to tell about the person you are throwing bones for. The ancestors are clever. When they talk to us, it feels natural and it is always clear what they are trying to tell us. Even the people we meet and befriend, the people we feel drawn to, those we want to help, we will always benefit from some interaction with those people. The ancestors always have something in mind. They help us make the right decisions, do the right things. They attract us to the right people.'

In the course of visiting and interviewing healers it became clear to me that my preference was to be with the healers and have another person take photographs and slides as necessary. I spoke with professional photographers in the region but was disappointed. The photographers had been in southern Africa for years and did impressive work. Several had photographed the larger, more public traditional ceremonies. They were excited by my access to this group of healers and recommended I speed up the interviewing process. They said my access was unusual and I must act quickly lest the healers change their minds. My intuition said no professional photographers, do the photography myself and consider some amateurs.

I told the photographers my decision and went back to work. A month later I happened to mention my experience to a healer I was visiting in a remote area. She smiled and said that explained why the ancestors were keeping one particular photographer away from them at this time. She said that she and her fellow healers were getting a message from their ancestors that I was not to worry about photographs. My photographs would be fine and there were two friends from America who would help me if I needed them. Several weeks after that visit, I ran into one of the professional photographers. He was having difficulty finding a group of healers. He knew where they lived, had even visited there in the past but he couldn't quite get there. It was maddening. He would begin to drive to their place then lose his way and become disorientated. He said it was 'the craziest thing'.

During the Christmas holidays business in southern Africa closes down for as long as six weeks. During the Christmas break of 1992, a friend asked to accompany me on a visit to PH Mntshali. Albert Cohn, a Peace Corps volunteer from Tennessee, taught joinery at a remote high school. Albert was one of those special friends who quickly become a member of the family. Since our visits were infrequent we looked forward to the long ride to PH's homestead. Albert soon began talking of losing his father two years earlier when he was violently murdered. Without knowing it, Albert had chosen to visit a healer who had success asking the ancestors to help bring closure between a patient and a loved one who had died, particularly in cases of sudden death.

PH greeted us both warmly and without hesitation threw bones for Albert. The experience was positive but very intense. PH then took me aside and said it was a good thing I was driving home so Albert could 'enjoy the closeness of the ancestors a bit longer'. On the way back I felt as if I was trying to get Albert's feet back on the ground. Somehow this experience had moved along the healing process for Albert and his father. We laughed and shared our experiences all the way back to Mbabane.

· 5 ·

Voice of the ancestors –
a healer possessed

lbert and I also discussed his doing some amateur photography with me and the healers. He was interested, but we both agreed to also ask Jill Lapato, a Peace Corps volunteer teaching physics at his high school. Part of my brain was racing to understand why I would want Jill with me at the healers. I had met Jill only once and wasn't comfortable with her. I kept thinking that such a special experience should be shared with a close friend or colleague. An electrical engineer from Boston, Jill was openly sceptical of my work. Her humour had an edge to it which I didn't always understand. I knew I didn't want to persuade Jill to come with me. Yet, I felt absolutely sure she should be asked. Even stranger, I knew it was Jill and not Albert that was to be the main person to help me.

Jill was in the States for the holidays. On her return she remained sceptical but found herself compelled to work with me. She, Albert and I agreed on some ground rules and scheduled our first visit together. As the ancestors would have it, Albert was unable to join us. Jill and I went out to a healer training site. It was a bright, sunny day but the trainer was not in. The trainees were unusually lively with their teacher gone. Jill and I were able to play around with our cameras. We were all comfortable with each other by the end of the visit and agreed to come back when the trainer returned. Jill was full of questions and probed at great length on the ride home. I didn't want to win anyone over to believing in or even understanding the healers. I didn't want to interpret their actions or their words. I just wanted someone to take the pictures for me. I wanted it to be easy. The second time Jill came out with me, an experience forever changed the nature of our relationship and her perspective on the healers.

We were scheduled to visit Khumbulile Mdluli in Ntfojeni on a Saturday morning. Again, Albert was not available. The drive up through the mountains was beautiful and soothing as always. Jill was agitated. One question followed another. What did I think about this? How could I explain that? What really goes on with these healers, isn't it all just superstition? I began to lose my patience. Perhaps I had made an error in judgement.

On top of it all, I didn't like Saturday visits. They were the busiest day for the healers, with patients travelling great distances for an appointment. It was no different at Khumbulile's that day. I felt guilty that we were taking time away from Khumbulile's patients, yet she seemed genuinely pleased to see us. I introduced her to Jill. She welcomed Jill warmly and then took me aside. I said nothing to Khumbulile about my discomfort with Jill but she spoke softly and directly to me, 'This woman has a good spirit. She will be helpful. You have been directed by the ancestors to bring her to me today. This is all proper. Now it is between the ancestors and Jill. You relax. You have done your part. That is all you need to know.' I felt an instant relief. Everything was as it should be and better yet, it was out of my hands.

Khumbulile promised to squeeze me in for our interview after her last patient. While waiting, we wandered around the homestead for much of the morning letting Jill get a feel for the place. Seeing Jill in action, so unobtrusive and respectful, made me glad she was there. Though a sceptic, Jill had a healthy respect for the Swazis and their traditions.

Khumbulile's last patient was a twenty-eight-year-old Swazi woman in western dress, a school teacher from the nearby town. This was her second visit to the clinic. Finally Khumbulile came out and said, 'The ancestors are coming. My patient and I give you and Miss Lapato permission to come inside while I conduct the consultation. You must move quickly, they are coming. You may take photographs of me and anyone present except for the face of my patient.' Jill and I were instantly excited and tense. Our senses snapped to attention.

Jill and I entered the one-room clinic with Khumbulile. The building was a traditional rondavel with a thatched roof. Khumbulile's clothing for healing rituals hung above what looked like an altar, the area where she greeted her most senior ancestors before beginning a consultation or treatment. There were bottles and jars of herbal medicines along the sides of the hut. People were filing in, the room was crowded. Khumbulile was moving more quickly than I had ever seen her move. I was not sure what to expect.

The energy level in the room was high. I felt as though we were at a celebration, something spiritual and happy, like a baptism or a marriage. Khumbulile's family members and close friends entered. There were fifteen women and children with us in the crowded hut. They were smiling and bringing in shakers and other percussion instruments. Jill and I sat directly across from them. Jill was handed a tin can with seed pods in it and instructed to shake it. Things were speeding up. A woman brought in a large, beautiful drum. Their drumming helped Khumbulile make and maintain contact with the ancestors.

The patient entered and sat with the women and children. These women were there to protect Khumbulile from any harm when she was possessed or in a trance, and to listen closely so they could later report to her all that had been said and done. Then Khumbulile's nine-teen-year-old nephew entered with a younger boy, and sat near Jill and me. They had been drinking marula wine for hours, and I wondered if they would be able to assist Khumbulile as she had asked.

Khumbulile knelt before a small altar-like arrangement, honouring the ancestors who were coming to her. She seemed oblivious to the activity around her. She pulled out a small honey pot, from her graduation ten years previously, added a very tiny amount of the honey to a herbal mixture and washed herself with this mixture. She then put on beads and ancestral clothing.

After putting on a skirt, beaded necklaces, and a bright red and white print tunic, Khumbulile finally covered herself with a black cloth, like a cape. She knelt over herbs burning on a shallow plate. Her eyes were glazed over. The ancestors were coming. I had never expected to witness a healer being possessed, and could not believe my good fortune.

Khumbulile began to speak in a man's voice, very low. It was strange but somehow not surprising at all. The ancestor introduced himself and greeted each of us in the room. Khumbulile took on a different personality. She was more aggressive, cocky, kind of a wise guy. I could not believe this change in her. The presence was bold. The nephew jumped up and ran out of the hut. He brought back drums. He, the younger boy and then a woman began beating these beautiful conga drums. The woman was exceptional. I was mesmerised. The sound was lively. I felt a deep, free feeling. The women were shaking tin cans with seeds inside while this man in Khumbulile sang.

Khumbulile moved around the room, abruptly stopping singing, then kneeling down in front of a bowl with the herbal wash mixture. She made a sound like a dog barking and her daughter gave her the bowl. She put the mixture on the goat tail stick she had in her hand. She stroked some of the mixture on her face with the goat tail and then did the same with the patient. More dancing, more singing, then the nephew and the other boy sprang into action. While singing, they placed a cloth over the head of the patient as she breathed in a herbal concoction burning on a shallow metal plate. The boys were clearly focused and moved quickly to assist Khumbulile.

Khumbulile began a spectacular dance as the drums beat more wildly. The dance steps and jumping were amazing, unbelievable choreography in such a cramped space. Never once did she touch anyone, bump into anything or lose her balance. I was astounded. I didn't want the dancing and the drum beating to stop. Looking up, I saw big smiles from the women across the room. They were watching me and we laughed together. Khumbulile was speaking in a language I had not heard before. The women said it was Sindzawe, an old language of the ancestors not spoken today. It was so evident that Khumbulile was a mouthpiece for this presence, this person. It was not a harmful presence. It did not feel threatening in the least. Some time later, the possession ended as abruptly as it started. The ancestor had gone. Khumbulile was exhausted. She sat back with the women and children and smiled. She did not remember what she had said or done. She remembered what treatment to give, but no other details of the ancestor's visit. Khumbulile turned to me with such sweetness and asked, 'So, how was it?'

Jill told me afterwards that she had been frightened during the whole process. I would not have stayed if I had sensed that she was in great distress or danger, but I chuckle now to realise how far out of my hands these encounters were. I was probably of little comfort during this particular experience. I knew we were safe but I was completely lost in the moment. I could not believe how great I felt.

When I had remembered, I had snapped off shots on my camera as fast as I could during the ceremony, nudging Jill from time to time to remind her to do the same. But Jill was often too busy taking in the scene. She didn't have time for cameras. It made me smile. When our slides were developed we noticed Khumbulile dancing without her tunic on. Neither of us had seen that happen. It would have been a noticeable movement, which we should have seen in such a small space. Jill and I were inches from Khumbulile the entire time and neither of us witnessed her removing this large garment. We scrutinised the slides afterwards and it left us completely baffled.

During Khumbulile's 'possession', we simply lost track of time. I did not check my watch going in, and afterwards Jill and I didn't know if it had taken ten minutes or an hour. We were at Khumbulile's homestead for a total of five hours. It is possible we were in the hut for as long as two hours. I found it completely absorbing. It seemed to affect everyone in the room the same way. It was a tremendous boost, such a joyful thing. Afterwards, neither Jill nor I were interested in the diagnosis. I know I was simply savouring the experience, the gift Khumbulile had just given me. The diagnosis was not important nor was it meant for me at that time.

I later learned that the patient's illness had started at work as if someone had 'come from behind'. She was feeling pains in her waist and had bladder problems. She was experiencing tiredness in her shoulders, as if someone had put something heavy on her. Some hair was coming out of her head. Her head hurt as if someone had actually pulled hair out. She wondered if the hair had been used in a witchcraft attempt. The ancestor, through Khumbulile, recommended a herbal treatment to be applied to a few shallow incisions on the patient's head. The ancestor advised that the herbal medicine would go to the rest of her body and clear up the pains. The ancestor cautioned that the patient's children would also suffer from this illness unless the patient was treated immediately. In a follow-up with Khumbulile, the patient reported the treatment had been successful.

After leaving Khumbulile's that day we gave the patient a lift into town. She was very calm and happy. She praised Khumbulile and said repeatedly how grateful she was to live near such a gifted healer. Soon after we left the patient, Jill and I pulled over to the side of the road. I had packed a cooler of sandwiches and cold drinks. We opened the back of the Land-Rover, ate and listened to the quiet around us. It was difficult to speak. I thought about the ride up and sensed a great change between Jill and myself. There was a comfortable silence. Jill had no questions. We were both full of wonder. I knew then that Khumbulile had been correct when she said I was just the vehicle to bring Jill to her and the other healers. I had no other responsibility than to honour Jill's part in this process. From that moment on, I knew Jill and I would have greater tolerance for one another having gone through that experience together. It was a gift to us from Khumbulile and her ancestor.

Healer graduation – the final test

raduation is not a ceremony to acknowledge completion of study, as it is in western societies, but in fact is the most difficult test endured during the healer's training. A few months into my healer visits, I expressed an interest in attending a graduation ceremony. The healers received this with an unusual reserve. They agreed I should attend a graduation but were not sure when. In time a training group was identified and a graduation date confirmed. The THO staff assisting me in Swaziland made the proper communications only to find the group graduated a week early. Notice of another graduation came up but the telephone lines to my house were not working and THO could not get word to me in time. After a few more of these incidents, I gave up. For whatever reason, I was not to attend a graduation.

The healers finally shared a story with me that explained their caution. The graduation ceremony is the most exotic and primitive experience the healers go through and therefore the most colourful to westerners. Taken out of context, however, the graduation does not paint an accurate picture of the healers' day-to-day life nor respectfully show their significant contribution to primary health care. Some twenty years ago, the healers approved a request from an anthropologist to attend and film a graduation ceremony. Afterwards the anthropologist approached the Swaziland government for an endorsement to distribute the film upon his return home. Seeing the film in isolation disturbed the government officials. They believed it would not represent the healers in their true light. The government withheld its endorsement and refused to support any distribution of the film.

Many of the older, senior healers remembered this. They were concerned that my own experience had been so positive, attending the graduation ceremony might disturb me. I valued this group's perspective and had no desire to go against their wishes. So it was with great surprise that months later I learned Khumbulile was organising a visit to a graduation for me. Khumbulile was highly regarded. If she had been given permission to proceed, they must have believed I was ready. The fact that Khumbulile, with whom I shared a strong connection, was the person chosen to coordinate the event gave me a great sense of comfort.

Swazi graduation ceremonies always take place in winter, June through August. A plant important to the ceremony matures at this time. Khumbulile told me I could bring Albert and Jill, my amateur photographer friends, who had earned the respect of the healers. Khumbulile believed they would handle the day with sensitivity. As the date approached I began to have strong thoughts that two friends from Johannesburg should also attend. I discussed this with Khumbulile who believed these thoughts were an order from my ancestors. I extended the invitation to Jacci and Anne Marie not knowing if they would actually make the trip but feeling I had done my part.

On 31 July 1993 we attended the graduation of five trainees, all women, who studied under Khumbulile's own master trainer. The Ñtrainer's homestead was in rural Swaziland, a stone's throw from the Mananga Border of South Africa. On the morning of the graduation, I drove from my house in Mbabane to Ntfojeni to collect Khumbulile. Jacci, an American working in Johannesburg and Anne Marie, a South African kinesiologist, came as observers. Albert and Jill accompanied us as photographers. We left Mbabane at 4 am. It was dark, cold and foggy. Visibility was nil. I couldn't see a car in front of me. We crawled along for nearly two hours.

Arriving at Khumbulile's, we learned that her sister Olga would also be coming. I was distressed, there wasn't enough room. I had written specifically to tell Khumbulile that my car would be packed full and we could take no extra passengers. The letter had never arrived. Khumbulile explained that her ancestors would soon be 'coming out'. When in trance, she would not be able to communicate with us and needed Olga not only as her protector but also to interpret the day's activities and events to us. Khumbulile was so calm. She said space was not a problem, we would manage. Khumbulile sat in the front seat with me, while Jacci and Olga squeezed with great effort into the back of the Land-Rover, propped up on bags, jackets and food.

We arrived at the graduation site just before 8 am. The sun had just come up. It was cool. People at the homestead had blankets wrapped around them and were sitting near an open fire. There were a few people there, maybe thirty total. The trainees or healer initiates were sitting in their hut quietly. We were told they had been up all night dancing and had just stopped to rest. They had been calling their ancestors and had been 'possessed' most of the night. They were physically and emotionally exhausted.

I noticed a set of horns on the thatched roof of the initiates' hut. I had seen horns like this on many of the healers' traditional clinics. Khumbulile explained that they came from an animal that was slaughtered to honour the ancestors. The animal was cooked and a feast prepared to honour the ancestors that guide and speak through the matron. Thanks is given for the assistance the ancestors provide. The horns are then placed on the hut where healing or teaching of healers takes place.

I had expected a large crowd, maybe hundreds of Swazis and many expatriates, Europeans with cameras. This was a very special ceremony; the trainer – 'matron' they called her – was widely respected. If I could see only one graduation before I left Swaziland, I was told, this should be the one. It was an honour to be invited.

Khumbulile was a special graduate of this matron, and was treated with respect by all. She had spoken with her trainer over several visits to gain permission for us to attend. Khumbulile had no transportation and the matron was a day's travel from her own homestead. At that moment I appreciated what a major effort Khumbulile had made. We were treated royally, and allowed to move freely throughout the training compound. At one point we were even allowed to enter the initiates' hut.

I noticed a strong, pleasant odour from the fire when we arrived. It smelt of forests and bushveld, very musky. The fire was made from a special bark that serves as an incense. It burns over the crowd all day, each day of the graduation. This incense, though not a hallucinogen, is said to increase contact with the ancestors. Everything we witnessed that day, the dancing, chanting, drum beating, herb burning, muti drinking, had one common purpose, to increase the quality and the quantity of contact with the ancestors.

The day seemed to take me slowly away to another place in my mind and my emotions. I remember feeling very honoured and very calm in the morning. I wandered among the initiates and was always just inches away from them and the elder healers. At one point in the afternoon, I looked up from where I was standing and saw about a hundred people in the audience watching from a greater distance. I had not noticed these people arriving, they were in the background of my experience.

By the afternoon I could feel the energy of the gathering had increased, a momentum had built up. It is customary in Swaziland to pay employees once a month. This was pay weekend, the rowdiest weekend of the month. Many people in this growing crowd had been drinking traditional beer for hours. For a moment I felt nervous about my safety. I felt we stood out too much. Could we become targets for violence or abuse if the crowd took a nasty turn owing to the alcohol? The feeling passed through my body slowly. The next thing I knew I was once again feeling safe. I experienced a feeling of something like a cocoon wrapped around me. I didn't worry again.

Khumbulile went into trance ten minutes after we arrived at the graduation site. She went directly into the hut where the initiates stayed. We heard a deep voice, the voice of the man Jill and I had heard when Khumbulile was possessed at her clinic in Ntfojeni. She and the initiates, also in trance, came out of the hut dancing and shouting in their possessed voices. They all wore traditional clothing. Khumbulile led the dancing. They danced over to the matron, where they praised her and honoured her exceptional healing and training abilities.

The singing stopped, the ancestors left their bodies. All was dramatically and instantly quiet. The initiates were given beautiful headdresses made of bright fuchsia and purple feathers. After the possession ended Khumbulile and the others were silent: the ancestors had taken their voices.

The burst of energy from the dancing while Khumbulile and the trainees were possessed was intense. It was a short burst but I felt weak in my knees and sat down. I remember thinking, 'Oh good, now I can relax.' While resting, Khumbulile showed us a special stick that she had received during training. Today's trainees would also receive such a stick with rhino tail hair on the end of it. Muti is put on the end of the stick where the healer holds it. Around and covering this muti are small, special sea shells. This muti gives off a certain scent that enhances the ancestor's communication with her when she shakes the stick during her healing practice.

We had been resting only minutes when the initiates seemed to fly from the hut. I was caught off guard, adrenalin rushing through my body. There was frenzied chanting, loud drum-beating. The elder healers, all graduates of this same matron, joined the trainees in dancing.

The initiates were then each given a goat, identified by their ancestors to the matron. This goat, while still alive, had its throat slashed. The trainees then drank the blood from the goat, followed this with a herbal drink, and vomited immediately. After the vomiting, the trainees were given porridge to settle their stomachs and allow the ancestors to come to them more quickly. If the trainee was not able to vomit immediately, it was a sign that she had done something to dishonour the ancestors or had disobeyed them during training.

This particular test relates to the abstinence rule. The trainees are not allowed any sexual contact during their training, which can take up to three years. I noticed that just before this test, they were unusually nervous, sweating profusely and shaking.

I asked Olga: 'Why are they so nervous? What happens if they don't vomit?'

'They die,' Olga stated.

I was stunned by her calm matter-of-factness. I probed further and asked, 'Has it ever happened that a trainee has actually died because they have not passed this test?'

'Yes', she said.

Now I was nervous, and braced myself for what was to come.

Khumbulile remembers the day: 'Following this test for abstinence, I led the trainees to the river. They took the blood of their goat and put it all over their bodies. They kept it on about fifteen minutes. This is done by the river so they can easily wash it all off. It does not take long. It is during this time that the matron and her helpers were hiding the goat tails, fur, and other things. As we were coming up from the river, the ancestors were already guiding the trainees to find these objects.

'When the initiates went down to the river there was one who returned to the homestead by herself. During the time they were being tested, she did not vomit well. She started shivering. This was happening because she had done something wrong to the ancestors. She went down to the river to wash with the others but it was there she began to feel very dizzy. At the river, the initiates are given the red and leopard spotted skirt and other pieces of the traditional healer dress for the first time. This woman became dizzy and had to return, she did not receive her dress there. She had done something during training that was forbidden. Perhaps she met with a man. This is why the ancestors treated her like this at the graduation. They showed mercy on her because she did not die, but she was punished.

'When the trainees came back from the river, the elder healers had now hidden the individual bowls containing pieces of the goats used in the ceremony. The trainees had to immediately find the bowl containing bits of skin and hair from their exact goat. Their ancestors would tell them where these bowls were. Except for the one woman the ancestors were punishing – she had trouble finding the objects. During that test, it did not come easily to her like it did for the others. The ancestors were not happy with her. Everyone watching the ceremony, all the elders and the people from the community, they were now aware that the ancestors had moved away from her. They could see that the ancestors did not show her where the hidden items were. She felt very ashamed and embarrassed in front of the crowd that was watching. The other four trainees had no troubles. The ancestors stayed with them the entire time. They had no problems. The ancestors helped them to pass all their tests.

'The woman who had a difficult time must now go back to the ancestors and ask them to help her. The ancestors will tell her what she needs to do to reconcile with them. If she follows their instructions exactly, she will be right again. She will not be able to attract any patients until she clears this up with the ancestors. She must cleanse herself at the site of the trainer, after spending a month in the initiate hut, before she returns to her own community. Those who were at the ceremony, the graduation, they will doubt her abilities as a healer. And the older established healers who were there will not send clients to her. It will take her a long time to establish a practice.

'This is the way the ancestors punish you if you have done something wrong during training, if you have disobeyed the rules. The ancestors did finally help her to find the hidden objects at the ceremony, but now those in the audience doubt her abilities. There were some in the crowd who were watching this closely. They may not know it yet, but they will go into training to become a healer next year. They have learned something about what happens when you do not observe closely the rules of the training, the wishes of the ancestors. They will not forget.

'I did not see a graduation ceremony before I went into training myself, so I didn't know what to expect. It's a very difficult thing, this training – and then to go through the graduation! Just drinking from a container with herbs that must pass through you … it is difficult to just drink like a cow. We are given our drink in a bowl. We must go down on our hands and knees and drink like an animal. We are human beings but we must be so humble before our trainer and our ancestors during the training, and especially during the graduation. We drink a lot of medicine and it is bitter. It is not an easy thing. We vomit, and our voices change. It is not pleasant. It is not an easy test, to pass this graduation ceremony.

'After the two days of the graduation, the initiates must stay together in one room, in the initiate hut, for a period of one month. If they go out of the hut, their bodies must be covered completely. They do not talk to one another during this time, or to others in the homestead. If they want food, there are others in the homestead who will cook for them. They don't go out. They stay in there wearing the skin of the goat that they drank the blood of during graduation. Inside the room they will be fixing bones and horns of their goats from graduation, preparing them. These things will help them in their traditional healing practice. At the conclusion of the month in the hut, they will again be tested. They come out of the hut, go to the river and cleanse their bodies. Their trainer will hide these objects they have made. Their ancestors must come out and help them find these items one final time.'

Khumbulile recalls her own graduation: 'There were twelve trainees in my group. My graduation was in winter but we were not cold as long as the ancestors were with us. I wore the colours of this same trainer. My skirt was red with black leopard-like spots. This is the uniform you wear at graduation. Each trainer has his or her own uniform. You can tell where someone trained, who their trainer is, by this uniform. This uniform is determined by the ancestors. When we put on this cloth at the river we began speaking the ancient ancestral language, Ndzawe.

'The graduation lasted two days. I remember a hard test on the second day. We went down to the river and had to crawl back to the matron's homestead, one kilometre on our knees. We came up a steep hill from the river and over a rough dirt road, over stones and rocks. Mats were placed in front of us. We had to jump or hop, using only our upper bodies to go from mat to mat. It was a hard thing. Before that, we took more goats. We killed them, put them on our shoulders. The blood spilled out all over our bodies. Then the trainer and her helpers took a part from inside the goat. They mixed it with the blood and put it on our bodies. We went immediately to the river and washed ourselves. There, the ancestors came out. We spoke in their voices.

'Then a cut was made on our bodies. Most cuts we make in training are shallow, small cuts. On this day the cuts are deep and they bleed. Muti is rubbed into the cut. Only the muti that is for bringing out the ancestors, not any other kind of muti can be put into these cuts. Only the matron knows what type of muti to put in each cut of each initiate. The ancestors from the trainees are guiding her. The muti may vary from person to person. It all depends on what the ancestors advise.

'For me, the hardest part of the graduation was drinking the goat blood. I was convulsing, I was so scared to drink it. Up to that time, I didn't even eat goat meat. During that day, I was supposed to drink this goat blood and swallow some of the cooked goat meat. We cannot chew it, we must just swallow it. Then it is supposed to come right up, we should vomit it immediately. If it does not come out immediately then there is a problem and you have done something wrong like that woman in the training we saw. We have done something to dishonour the ancestors and we must find out what and make amends. We can even die as a result, if the ancestors wish.'

There were times during the ceremony that day, watching Khumbulile, watching the initiates, when I felt completely detached. Throughout the day I felt out of space and time. I couldn't judge how long we had been there. At one point, I told Jill and Albert that I was exhausted, feeling I needed to leave soon. At that point we had been there seven hours. It felt like it was late at night, yet it was only 3 pm. I was afraid it would be rude to ask Khumbulile to leave now. Ordinarily we would sit and wait for the matron to close the day's activities before leaving. I found Khumbulile giving my two friends from Johannesburg a consultation in one of the huts on the compound. Khumbulile surprised me by saying she and her sister were also ready to leave. As with the entire experience, we were completely in sync.

In taking our leave, we had to walk through the growing crowd. We waded through the people and got in front of the matron and her husband. We thanked them for the day and Khumbulile interpreted for us. I didn't understand all the strange and wonderful things that had happened around me, but I felt so content.

Khumbulile had told me my own contact with the ancestors would increase by simply observing the graduation. My protection from and connection with my ancestors would be evident. Witnessing the graduation had a profound impact on me. It was not until 15 September 1993, six weeks later, that I was able to write about the experience. I found it difficult to even discuss what it felt like to be there, the impressions and physical effect it had on me. Whenever I attempted to discuss the experience I would be filled with an intense joy. It was almost like an explosion. It was an experience I would never forget.

Part Two:
The Healers

Isaac Mayeng –
Tswana healer and international
researcher

saac Mayeng, of the University of Cape Town (UCT) Traditional Medicines Programme (Tramed), has been a practising sangoma for nearly twenty years. Raised in a western-orientated household with no exposure to traditional African herbs, Isaac began the study of western medicine at university in 1976. In 1978, to his own surprise, he accepted a spiritual calling to become a traditional healer and successfully completed a rigorous two-year training course. In 1984, Isaac was awarded a scholarship to attend the highly competitive pharmacy programme at the State University of New York in the United States. He went on to complete further work in medicinal chemistry and advanced organic chemistry. Since 1991 Isaac has been working with UCT to create a southern African network of researchers to explore the active agents found in the traditional herbal remedies.

UCT's Traditional Medicines' Programme has a database that centralises information on plant chemistry, toxicology and pharmacology. The core of the database consists of some 46 000 anecdotes and the results of in-house tests of 350 plant species. Medicinal plants are used widely by indigenous South African healers and are also used by the public for self care. In addition to being used for conditions recognised by modern medicine, the herbal treatments are used for magical, ritual and symbolic purposes and for treating 'traditional ailments'. The plants are usually used in raw form and are harvested in the wild. South Africa has a remarkable biodiversity with approximately 3Ä000 species of plants that are used as medicines. About 350 species are the most commonly used and traded throughout the country. Although there are no accurate figures available, the unregulated trade in crude medicinal roots, barks, bulbs and leaves is estimated to be worth R1 billion annually. The annual turnover for the top 35 crude herbal medicines in Gauteng Province alone is estimated to be R21 million. In addition to the information about the plants, Isaac stresses the importance of understanding traditional concepts of disease and traditional preventative, promotive and curative health strategies. The Tramed database also includes information on Zulu and Xhosa medicinal plants as well as information on traditional healers and oral tradition.

I was born in Kimberley on 13 July 1954. There were no traditional doctors in my family. My father and mother were school headmasters. They were western in their orientation towards medicine and did not use herbs or natural traditional treatments. I too did not believe in this traditional way of healing. In fact, I had planned to become a medical doctor. I studied at South Africa's University of the North but the student strikes of 1976 made it difficult to continue and I was forced to quit in 1977. I taught science and languages at Saint Bonaveld school while studying further science through the University of South Africa's correspondence courses.

'Early in 1978, out of the blue, I became very, very ill. I was experiencing the "sangoma sickness". My ancestors were trying to get me to accept this calling to traditional medicine. I refused. I consulted a variety of medical specialists but found no relief. Finally a visit to an old man in the town of Hershel in the former Transkei homeland brought me relief. I had seen this exact man in a vision and was told he would be my teacher. I trained under this man, this healer. I became his *thwasa* (in Zulu) or *mokoma* (in Setswana.) To qualify as a traditional healer under this master healer, the old man required me to experience and understand visions. Visions were already coming fast and steadily to me, especially in the first five months. While in training, the visions accelerated my learning and within two years, I was an inyanga, a sangoma.

'My trainer and his students are careful with the use of symbols and ceremony. I don't wear beads and outward signs of being a sangoma in normal everyday life. This is considered holy attire, used only for the purpose of healing. It is similar to priests who only use certain stoles, scapulars, or the like, for certain ceremonies. For special and high ceremonies, they bring out special garments and symbols. It is important that traditional healers do not overuse or misuse our symbols of healing. They can be used in the wrong way and may lose their meaning and healing ability.

'Anyone can put on beads and pretend to be a sangoma. There are many pretenders these days. In some cases, the socioeconomic situation causes them, in desperation, to try to behave as if they are a sangoma. But they are playing with a complicated, special thing. They cannot succeed. Patients can be hurt by these type of people. A sangoma needs to know how medicines work. Healers must know their herbs thoroughly, what they are, levels of toxicity and dosage.'

There are many kinds of healers, but let me explain the two basic categories of healers I see in southern Africa. The first type is "called" to the profession. This person receives a powerful spiritual calling from the ancestors that is not easy to resist. Often they try to resist but become very ill. Different people experience different types of symptoms. Some get wounds that do not heal. Some go mad. Some get chronic diarrhoea. Some get migraine headaches or problems with eyes. The symptoms are varied, serious and can be life threatening.

'This group has the strictest code of conduct. These are the most spiritual of the healers, with the highest ethic. In training they work under a tutor. The training is very rigorous and challenges the trainee both physically and emotionally. We must adhere to certain rules during the training, certain foods we may not eat, we are not to hit a child or hurt a dog or cat, we are not to listen to loud music, nor have sexual relations, even with our marriage partner. We have to follow these do's and don'ts strictly in order for the training and our "call" to take hold properly.

'Like all members of this group of "called" healers, I believe in God. We believe in a power greater than ourselves, believe the ancestors are the go-betweens between ourselves and God. This is a deep, deep calling. We can never give up this calling, only in death. We did not choose to become healers, we were chosen, by God and our ancestors. We pray to our ancestors and God for clear guidance and we must follow that guidance. Our responsibility is as great as our healing gift. We can never harm. We can never kill.

'These are quiet people who do not ordinarily call attention to themselves. Being a "possessed" healer is an individual experience. It is not a group gift and cannot be orchestrated. It happens individually and the person is led to training. Some faith healers in South Africa enter into trance states as a group, becoming possessed, for example, in their churches. Well, it doesn't happen that way with us, the sangomas. For instance, when I was with my teacher, he and I would never be possessed at the same time. It happens individually and one at a time. God and the ancestors act in this way. They do not just come out to a group, all at the same time.

'The second general category of traditional healer can choose to train and study because of his or her interest and curiosity. They are more like technicians. They have no common code of conduct. There is no "contract" between themselves and a higher power, to heal and never harm. There is not a strong and binding belief that they are simply the messengers or the pipeline, the instruments, of the ancestors and God.

'Some of this group are only interested in the practice of herbs for the money it can earn them. They may be interested in herbs but later decide to do some other work. They can choose what to do with this knowÑledge of herbs. Some in this group even study herbs through correspondence or are taught in a school. Some gifted teachers are able to develop the abilities in this group, but these technicians never cross over to become the spiritually chosen people in the first group I described. They do not have this psychic ability, this clairvoyance, the contact with the ancestors. Some healers in this technician group may, for instance, have an ability to go into a trance and speak for the ancestors. They may take a three- to six-month training and even then, it may be a part-time training to develop this skill in fortuning. They may understand and study the use of some herbs, but they do not have a comprehensive view and understanding. They never cross over into the "possessed" or sangoma group.

'It is hard to demarcate the boundaries between healers. Like faith healers, they are operating with a limited ability, compared to the sangoma group. You must look at the parameters in which a healer works, to understand which group they belong in. There are some good healers in the "technician" group, they are just somewhat limited in their expertise and lack the deep spiritual "calling".'

'After my sangoma training, I didn't quite believe in my own gift but patients still found me. It seemed to me like magic that I could diagnose and heal. It was a bit unnerving and took some getting used to. I decided to return to teaching until I understood or became more comfortable with this healing ability. I taught mathematics to Form One up to Form Three. I even went to work for the mines. Still the patients continued to seek me out.

'It took me some time to adjust to this gift. It seemed so old fashioned to me, this traditional way. It did not suit my thinking. I found I could attend to many patients and while I was engaged in healing work, I did not tire because the ancestors worked through me. I was not actually exerting the energy. Like my teacher, a very, very old man today, who still can see patients non-stop, all day long, and be rejuvenated by it. A healer can have this metabolism. When I asked my trainer did he ever rest, he said, "Did God ever rest?"

'During this period of my life, some very strong force was causing me to read the Bible. I could only read the Bible. Whenever I tried to read other things, the newspaper, scientific publications, recreational reading, my vision would consistently blur. You know, when I was in training with this gifted old man, I was never, never once told that I should not be a member of a church or attend church services. In fact, I still have that same Bible sitting in my surgery even today.

'Something happened and this blurring of vision stopped suddenly in 1984. I could read again, newspapers, journals, anything, and I was offered an opportunity to study in New York. I entered the School of Pharmacology and was training to be a pharmacologist. It was a tough, tough group to join. In order to remain in this demanding programme, I had to maintain the highest level of study and performance. I even took additional, advanced courses in medicinal chemistry. I finally decided that the pharmacist certification would hamper or interfere with my ability to prescribe as a traditional healer because pharmacists can only administer, only dispense, not prescribe.

'The study of medicinal chemistry was interesting. If a person is allergic to penicillin, what actually happens in the body when they take penicillin and why? What are the antidotes? How and why do they work? How do bacteria become resistant to previously effective antibiotics? How does a virus mutate? This was so very interesting to me. However, the research in that area was completely drugs and chemical related, not natural medicines. At this point I began studying advanced organic chemistry.

'I completed this degree in America and returned to South Africa in 1989. I happened to notice an advertisement in the Johannesburg newspaper The Star, for a position with the University of Cape Town in the chemistry department. I applied and was chosen from hundreds of applications coming in from all over the country. Fortunately my studies, my research, were just right for what they wanted. I worked within the chemistry department for nearly two years before I again began to feel that chemistry was not right for me. I submitted my resignation only to be informed that UCT pharmacology department was developing a traditional medicines research programme. I joined the effort in 1991 and remain challenged by this exciting work today. I also have my own private herbal medicines production and supply business, as well as a traditional healing practice.'

It is good that I know both worlds, the western science, the chemistry, and the herbal, the traditional. Now I am learning that I must know more about the politics of the traditional healer professional groups. There can be such fireworks between these groups. I have been called on to chair meetings when the emotion between the various groups becomes too heated. I am often identified as the neutral party to get the discussions back on the track. I am more or less conversant in what is happening in the traditional healers' constituency.

'I know the leaders of the most prominent South African healer associations. It happens that government, pharmaceutical companies, research institutes, and other groups want me to address or brief these professional groups on certain issues for them. I myself do not belong to any association. This allows me to remain neutral. I can offer honest, constructive criticism and maintain my peace of mind.

'For example, a pharmaceutical company will want to understand the market that uses traditional remedies. Well it is a huge market. There will be stiff competition for it. It is an international market as well because Germany, the USA, Australia and others are interested in using these natural African remedies. The companies are positioning themselves with the healers. There are companies developing medical aid schemes for users of traditional healers' services. They want to know how to access the healers. This is yet another effort to understand the various constituencies of the healers. These groups are interested in the markets the healers represent, not necessarily the healers themselves.

'The government needs to be doing more to understand how the healers and the medical side can better complement one another and better serve the patient. For instance here is a simple thing. If a patient is taking antibiotics, let's say he is to take twenty tablets over seven days. On the fifth day he is feeling much better and stops taking the tablets. However, soon his illness returns and with worse symptoms this time. That person consults his traditional healer at the same time as the doctor. If the healers understand about antibiotics, they will reinforce the instructions of the doctor and explain why it is necessary to complete the course. There are so many ways the healer can help. Just as a doctor needs to recognise signs that the patient is also consulting a healer and understand how to complement the traditional treatment without creating a toxic reaction in the patient. In some instances, no additional medical treatment should be given until the course of the current traditional treatment is finished. These things must be understood across the two sides.

'I have my doubts about these primary health care and medical aid programmes that want to incorporate the traditional healers. There are so many impostors amongst the healers. How will they screen and select only those true, well-qualified and experienced healers? Who are the healers they register? What is their level of education? It's enough for healers and doctors to refer to and consult with one another now – but we are not ready, and it may never be appropriate, for the two to merge. True and gifted traditional healers are not against working with the nurses and the doctors. We all must understand the various issues involved, and there are many. This cooperation is just going to take time to sort out.

'Some healers think that if they cooperate with the medical side, then the government will pay them a salary. Well, that can never happen. How would the government choose these healers to be on their payroll? No, it won't happen. These issues have to be dealt with carefully. There need to be checks and balances in such cooperation. At the national level, the element of power and greed comes into play quickly. The issues are economic, political, technical issues. It is very complicated when you begin to think of institutionalising the cooperation at the national level.

'We need to address the role of capacity building and enabling here. The doctors need to learn so much to understand the healers. The healers themselves need constant skill upgrading. In incorporating the healers into some national system of health care, there must be bridges built between them in an institutional way. There must be a separate registering body, not falling under the Medical and Dental Council. It must be a new, independent body that knows exactly what its role, mission and limitations are. Plus attitudes have to change, must change amongst the medical people. The true, experienced healer must not be seen as subservient to, or less than, the medical people. I know this is all difficult, but there are always solutions to a problem.

'If government decides that the healers must sort out these issues for themselves – well, I can understand taking that position. However, the healers need and deserve to be given assistance and support in their own process. Now at the personal, individual levels, these collaborations between medical and traditional practitioners have been happening for years in South Africa. The healer and the doctor are serving the same community. Both are focused on the patient. There are no politics involved. They have found their own solution. They respect one another as equals. Doctors and healers are equally important to the patient. They are simply health care practitioners coming from different but complementary perspectives.'

I cannot emphasise enough the importance of the traditional healers in the role of primary health care in South Africa. They are not only the primary contact, but the secondary and tertiary points of contact for health care services in South Africa. I envision the existing parallel systems of traditional and medical health care delivery systems continuing in South Africa, but with increased and better referrals between the two. The Aids epidemic in southern Africa might be just the emergency that draws these two systems together, though they have some problems to work out.

'Many traditional healers have done credible experimentation with herbal remedies for HIV/Aids but their efforts have not been well documented, or in some cases, documentation was done in cooperation with a medical or scientific person who then presented the data as his or her own. Traditional healers have become sceptical of sharing their information, experience and data. Some healers have found their work published in journals under the name of their medical colleagues, with no mention that they are the ones who designed and administered the treatment, and kept the records of patient progress. Many healers feel, and rightly so, that their work has been stolen.

'For instance, there was a case of a traditional healer in Kenya who was said to be having some good results reversing HIV. This was amazing and hopeful, especially considering the affordability of the herbal medicines he used. He was reluctant to come forward with his data as he also had some misgivings about the ethics of the modern scientific community.

An international conference of healers, doctors and researchers was to be held in Nairobi and he agreed to present his findings there. The night before he was to present his studies, he was murdered in Nairobi. All traces of the data he had with him, and the additional documentation left behind in his village, all vanished.

'Whenever there is a natural plant growing freely which improves or cures a given disease, the pharmaceutical industry and the scientific industry will prevent this herb from being widely distributed. The rules of the game demand that the active ingredients in the plant be isolated, reproduced, synthesised, then packaged in such a way to sell to a mass market. Now the traditional healer is paying a great cost for the very medicine that was given to him in nature. No, he believes he is better off to use his treatments and keep results quiet. He serves his clients, his community. He shares findings with only trusted colleagues. It goes no further – and you can understand why.

'Even with difficulties such as these, I remain very optimistic about traditional healers and people of science working together and think the issue of Aids will go forward to test the waters of cooperation between the medical and the traditional practitioners. It won't be easy for certain doctors who have, sadly, hard-set negative attitudes about the traditional healers. Without the traditional healers on their side, the medical profession will simply lose this fight against Aids. They need the traditional healers more than the traditional healers need them.'

Nomsa Dlamini –
national activist, nurse and
sangoma of Soweto

Forty-five years old and one of the hardest working single mothers I have come across, Nomsa has the zest of a woman half her age. She aptly describes herself as a 'bridge' between the modern and traditional health sectors. Her confidence and enthusiasm seem to know no bounds. I have seen her in action at her traditional healing clinic and beside me at meetings with management staff of South Africa's Department of Health. She is consistently compassionate and articulate about how best to serve the health needs of a region steeped in a rich healing culture.

'My mother, a Xhosa, was born in the township of Sophiatown in Johannesburg. My father was a Swazi soldier. My father decided to move to South Africa after meeting my mother on holiday. My mother was a beautiful woman and my father knew he must marry her. It was unusual for the man to leave his home to follow his wife. Usually the woman goes to the man's family, but my mother had no sisters and brothers and my father was very fond of his mother-in-law. My family was one for mixing, Xhosas, Tswanas, Swazis, all marrying together. My grandmother was a Motswana, born in Gabane, Botswana. My grandfather from my mother's side was a sangoma. He was the first ancestor to contact me. He is still the strongest one helping me today.

'I was born an identical twin on 21 February 1952, in Orlando East, Soweto. My sister passed away in 1954 at two years old. My parents told me what happened but I couldn't understand it, until my sister explained everything to me in a dream. On the day she died, my father was driving home in a truck. I was sleeping inside the house. My sister was awake and went outside. My father didn't see her in the driveway and he ran over her. When I think of this accident, I imagine how horrible my father's pain must have been. He suffered for years from this accident and nearly committed suicide. This was a terrible burden.

'I was schooled in Orlando East. As a child I had no idea that I would become a healer, though I did dream a lot, seeing such things as a person who was going to die. I would tell my parents, "Something is going to happen." I would pray for the person in my dream. My parents, especially my mother, knew I was going to become a healer. She became a healer and my father too. They had a practice from home like me. Many patients came to them to be healed.

'Like me, my mother was a nursing sister before she became a healer. She left nursing in 1959. From 1959 until 1984, when she passed away, she was an active healer. When I was a child, I thought I wanted to become a nurse. At home I was taking care of sick people, praying for sick people. When a person had a problem, I used to listen, really listen to them, I so wanted to help.

'Nursing training was interesting and I enjoyed it. The information came easily to me. I nursed for 15 years at Baragwanath, the largest hospital in Soweto, and in a hospital in the Vaal area. I was happy being a nurse and I was good at it. I especially liked working with children. During these years, I would advise patients to consult a traditional healer if the medicine prescribed for them at hospital was not effective. In certain cases, a herbal medicine, a natural traditional treatment, proved to be better for the person, for the illness. At that time, medical institutes and doctors did not have any understanding of the traditional health system. Understandably, they did not allow any such medicines or healers in their hospitals. I used to take some herbs from my mother to my patients. I knew what herbs would complement the patients' medical treatments. I knew how to avoid a toxic reaction. And always, I prayed for my patients.

'My mother used to say to me, "I don't want you to go into this traditional work. Being a healer is a heavy responsibility and you will suffer. You will lose everything." My mother wished me to become a medical doctor to avoid the hard life of healing. At that time, traditional healers were not respected. The public confused healers with witch-doctors and treated them badly. My mother was a great woman. She advised me well and wanted me to make a difference, to make a contribution in whatever work I chose.

'My medical training is very helpful. A healer can be very, very gifted but at times it is necessary to confer with a doctor, when a medical treatment becomes the appropriate intervention. Without this training, it is not easy to speak with the medical side or trust that medical treatment can be a good thing. If a traditional healer can speak the language of the doctors and nurses, can understand their orientation, cooperation becomes a very good thing. That ability to name a correct part of the anatomy, medical practitioners appreciate that. Healers with training and practice in western medicine bring something extra to their work. We are bridges between the two worlds, between the traditional and the medical.

'The ancestors "tell" the healer exactly what is wrong with the patient. It is different than listening through a stethoscope, finding clues and putting them all together to form an opinion. We are shown the exact nature of the problem. That is how we are able to describe exactly what you are feeling, what symptoms you are experiencing before you even speak. No one can do that, no matter how learned you are, no matter how brilliant your medical practice. No, we are talking about a gift, a healing gift from the ancestors and God, an extra insight, a special knowingness. In South Africa there are thousands of traditional healers, yet not all are well qualified with this gift. Maybe only one hundred are masters, this high level of gifted healer. We are few in this category.'

While I was working as a nurse, I became ill, for no apparent reason. I suspected this sickness was the "sangoma illness". I did not want to become a traditional healer, but also knew it was important to honour the ancestors and take the sangoma training. This also seemed my last hope for curing my suffering. In 1978 the illness started with horrible, constant migraine headaches. It lasted until 1986, when I finally started my healer training.

'The headaches were coming every day. When the headache started, I would feel drowsy, then nauseous. I would start shaking and weakening.

I couldn't tolerate the least noise and needed a quiet place to be alone. Tablets to relieve the pain were no longer working. Only when isolated from other people could I rest and feel better. My supervisors at the hospital were concerned about my health but did not want me to take this sangoma training because I was intelligent. I worked well and they didn't want to lose a good nurse to traditional healing. They discouraged me from doing the training. With all my pain and suffering, I nearly became mentally disturbed. It was so upsetting that in 1985 I nearly killed myself and my children. I knew then that I had no choice but to undergo the sangoma training, for my own and my family's sake.'

I dreamt about the place I was to go for training but when I woke, I didn't know where it was or who to contact. I even had a dream where I was shown herbs to take, but I didn't know where to get these types of herbs. I heard that there were plenty of herbs and healers doing business on Jeppe Street in downtown Johannesburg, so I went there. When I arrived, I saw a man standing by the door to his shop. He called to me, "Why are you wasting your time? Your ancestors told me that you will come here, that I should help you." I thought this person was a thug who wanted money from me. He was an African man dressed all in white, looking just like a doctor. He was very neat. He gave me his telephone number and said, "Call me. You are going to need me." He was a sangoma, but he didn't look like one.

'Two months later I met another sangoma. I told him about my encounter with this man on Jeppe Street. The sangoma said, "Let us slaughter a goat to the ancestors and ask them to please remove this calling from you." I did as he instructed. We honoured the ancestors, we slaughtered the goat. You know what happened after that? The sickness became worse! Now the ancestors had lost their patience with me. Every day now I was crying and suffering.

'I was not able to think clearly. I gave away my money and valuables. I was left with nothing. I thought, "I am dying now." I wrote a suicide letter. I said, "I am suffering. I am not responsible for my actions. Let me take my life and my children's' life, to spare them the suffering." There was a railway station near my house. When the train came, I planned to stand there with my children, on the rail. In 1986, after writing this suicide letter, I put it under my mattress. After I was dead, people would read it and understand my state of mind.

'Throughout this time I continued to dream of a place I must go for training. Finally, I was shown a place in Swaziland. I was also shown a woman. "See that woman? Do you know her?" the voices in the dream say. "That woman is going to help you but she is a very, very cruel woman. You must be patient with her. She will help you."

'I decided to go back to that man in the white jacket. I went downtown and there he was, still standing in the same spot. He saw me and said, "Today you are going to take a train to Swaziland." I said, "How do you know that I am coming to tell you that?" He said, "I was expecting you to come and be ready for training. I know this thing." I wanted to start my training in July 1986, but I delayed.

As soon as I made my decision to accept this training, my headaches immediately stopped. The horrible pain just stopped. It was a tremendous relief. I thought, "Perhaps this calling is finished now. I can just return to my normal life." I didn't return to the man as I had promised. I stayed away one month. In August, the headaches came back and I was violently ill. I said, "I will go to training. I will do anything to stop this pain." My sister agreed to care for my children during my absence. My sisters and brothers were very worried about me.

'I went back to this man, who again was patiently waiting for me to return. I told him about the woman in my dream. He listened and took a photograph out of his pocket. He showed it to me and asked, "Do you see the woman in your dreams?" There was the exact woman I had dreamed about! He said, "You will find this woman in Nkulungwane, Swaziland, just over the Oshoek border." The man then took me to the woman, who was his wife. She is also a sangoma, Lizzie Nkosi, and her husband is Lazerus Nkosi. Lizzie is still training sangomas today under Lazerus's supervision. In this case, the husband is the more gifted healer.

I stayed with Lizzie for three months. Usually it takes one to two years for such training. However mine was an unusual situation. My ancestors were teaching me through dreams. They showed me many things like the throwing of bones in my dreams. I was learning fast, day and night, nonstop. I had also learned much from my parents in their healing practice. My mother was so patient, very open, like a friend, like a trainer. I miss her a lot. Today my mother comes to me in my dreams and visions. She tells me who and when a patient is coming, how I must help them, what types of treatments, what types of herbs to use. She is a great help to me.

'My training and initiation was very traditional. I had to slaughter the goat, drink blood, find hidden things through divination, all those typical things. I slaughtered the goat in Swaziland and the cow here in South Africa, in Soweto. The cow was hidden from me and I had to find it through my ancestors. The day before I was to come home, the ancestors showed me in a dream very clearly where the cow would be hidden. It was not difficult for me. People were surprised to see me as a sangoma when I returned home. They had seen me helping in my parents' practice and working as a nurse at Baragwanath Hospital. Now, they had to get used to this new idea, me as a traditional healer.

'When I finished training I decided to resign from nursing. The very first day that I opened my own healing practice, patients were coming to me. I was busy all the time. I had no time to continue nursing. My husband, the father of my three children, passed away in 1994. He was very supportive of my work in traditional healing. While I was training he came to Swaziland to see me. He was such a good man. He was a Zulu from Natal. Through my healing practice, I managed to provide for my children. My son studies in environmental health at Wits Technikon, my younger sons are at private schools. I am a single parent but I look after us well. My oldest son wants to change to medicine at university. He is the next one taking to this area of healing and health.'

When I trained to be a sangoma, I often gathered the trainees and healers to discuss how we might organise and work together. I would say, "You know there are burial schemes where we help each other if someone dies. Why don't we open a scheme where sangomas can help each other?" This group had no experience in these matters and knew little on the business side. I was good at organising a clean clinic, organising a tidy traditional pharmacy; I had ideas on how to run a practice, had some good business ideas. I helped them with those things.

'Now as I train new healers, I teach my *thwasas* how to keep their books, how to keep a clinic tidy and hygienic. All herbs are labelled, good detailed records of patients and treatments are kept. I also impress upon the students that they must never go beyond their instructions from the ancestors — for instance, if a healer is asked to see a patient but has a bad feeling about them. The healer must never overrule the feeling the ancestors are giving her because she needs the money a patient may bring. If so, there will be problems of some sort. Traditional healers must be strict in listening to the ancestors, following their instructions.

'Over time I was meeting with many healers throughout South Africa. We decided we wanted a national organisation that could eventually be recognised by the government. In this way, the Traditional Medical Practitioners Organisation was formed in 1993. In 1994, the Icy Hot Company donated R30Ã000 to sponsor a two-day conference. We invited healers from all over South Africa, everyone was welcome. We aimed to form an umbrella body for the many smaller organisations; we wanted to benefit all the traditional healers. We hoped to form one voice with which to speak with the government, the private sector and the international donors. In our efforts we visited all the nine provinces. In 1995 we visited our MEC, Mr Masondo, who asked us to organise ourselves further. We attempted to do this but not all existing healers or healer organisations wanted to form this one voice. We were not discouraged, as we could see the benefit of such a union of healers. We continued going up and down, all over the country, talking with our colleagues, the healers.

'On 27 March 1996, we went to Parliament to speak about legislation to recognise the healers. As a result of that briefing, we are taking a national roll call for all the traditional healers interested in having our own council, our own registrar. On 26 October 1996 we met in Venda to discuss this legislation, the progress of the continuing roll call. In Venda, we formed a statutory body with healers from all regions who will address the constitutional issues of such a council of healers and a proper registrar. This group can advise government and clearly say what our standards are. I am one of six on the executive committee who give time to manage this process of the healers.

'A registrar for traditional healers will help to regulate standards for the healers and determine minimum qualifications and acceptable training. We would like our own person in Parliament as well, to represent the healers' constituency. We need a Minister of Traditional Healing to present our case in the southern African region and internationally. We want to see South Africa providing leadership on health issues and the cooperation between traditional and western medical practitioners. We want to have conferences and other types of communication between the healers and the medical side. We want to be able to ask questions, work out our problems and share our successes.'

Nana Makhanya –
government Aids counsellor and
traditional healer

I was intrigued by Nana Makhanya and her colleague, Heidi van Rooyen, a clinical psychologist. Theirs is an interesting collaboration, as Nana Makhanya, full-time government HIV/Aids counsellor and project manager, is also a well-known traditional healer. Nana also worked with Rose Smart, Director of South Africa's National Aids Programme, when they were both in Pietermaritzburg. Together they provided HIV/Aids training to 250 traditional healers in KwaZulu Natal.

Today, Heidi, Nana and the entire Pietermaritzburg Aids Training, Information and Communication Centre (ATICC) accept that the traditional healers are vital to their programme. They also believe that the healers can be critical participants in research programmes, especially in data collection and field work. Community members trust the healers and feel free to give them genuine information, which is not always the case with medical professionals. The healers often stimulate certain cultural and traditional values which help to reduce HIV/Aids by helping youth to internalise mores related to sexual practices. Many of the healers trained in HIV/Aids prevention also minimise the risk of infection of both the mother and the baby, as well as the traditional birth attendant herself. There was no doubt that the traditional healers formed an important component of the multi-disciplinary team approach to HIV/Aids prevention in the KwaZulu-Natal region of South Africa.

Nana's life in healing has not always been so well accepted. A fervent Catholic, Nana was shunned following her sangoma training. Her healing reputation overcame even this obstacle and in November 1996, a ceremony was held at her church. She was fully recognised as a traditional healer and, in her sangoma garb, welcomed back as a full member of the church. Nana says that the Catholic Church now includes a section on traditional healing in its training programmes for future priests.

Belonging to a western church and practising an ancient African healing form is not a contradiction in Nana's complex set of beliefs. In her government job, she dresses like any other professional, but when home she changes to traditional clothes for her healing work. Nana prays before she begins consulting with her patients. She asks God to send her ancestors, her guardian angels. These ancestral spirits tell her of peoples' problems and guide her to a remedy. When talking of the importance of healing, Nana says, 'Because of my calling, I am only allowed the power of good. I am not a witchdoctor. Yes, I know there are sangomas who will cause harm but I will not. I only help people. My ancestors – my angels – allow no other way.'

I t was difficult to follow this traditional way. My family and my friends were all western-educated people who did not support my choice. When I was ten years old, I started having dreams about gathering herbs, but I didn't tell anyone. My parents were strict Roman Catholics who believed all problems could be solved through prayer. So I prayed, but the dreams didn't stop. As I grew older I began to know when things were going to happen. Even with all these funny things happening to me, I never once imagined that I would become a traditional healer. It wasn't something my family knew anything about. It was completely foreign to us.

'Then my grandmother died and strange things started happening. I couldn't concentrate when I tried to study. At times my sight would just go. Everything went black in front of my eyes. These problems continued for years. In 1987, I began to feel people's problems. If they were nervous, I started feeling nervous. If they had pain in their tummy, I began to feel this same pain. I decided then to become an *umthandazi,* a faith healer. This type of healing through prayer and using holy water seemed to suit my faith and upbringing. But still I didn't feel settled and my problems didn't go away.

'It was much later, when I was pregnant again and kept having problems, that my friend took me to a traditional healer. The healer said my grandmother wanted me to become a sangoma. My problems would only stop, he said, when I answered the call. That really surprised me because this grandmother was such a strong and correct follower of the Catholic Church. When she was alive, we used to tease her and say, "Gran, you should have been a nun." She had no belief in these traditional things.

'About that time, I had visions that frightened me. I was in a relationship with a chief in the town of Richmond near Pietermaritzburg. The visions were showing me terrible violence that would come to his people. These events actually took place. I continued to know things as before, where people had been, what they had said, what they had done. Sometimes I visited other faith healers looking for help with dreams I didn't understand. Unfortunately, I found these people were jealous. Instead of helping me, they wanted to weaken my power. I began to think that maybe I really was meant to answer this call. I had heard the sangoma training was too expensive and I didn't know anyone to train under. So I continued with my studies in HIV/Aids prevention, my faith healing practice, and even worked in the South African elections during 1994.

'One day my eldest daughter rang me from Johannesburg. (By this time I was thirty-four years old, a single mother of four and already a grandmother.) My daughter was very ill and as a last hope, she had seen a traditional healer. I had never met this healer and my daughter had not spoken to him about me. Even so, he told my daughter that if I did not answer this call to become a sangoma, her health would not improve. I remember it was about a week after the elections in 1994 and I had just been paid for my work. Suddenly my grandmother was saying to me, "Don't you have the money now? Don't you think the person your daughter saw is the one to train you? Isn't this what you have been waiting for?" That was the final sign for me.

'This same traditional healer became my senior trainer. He taught me about herbs, diagnosis, treatment and consultation, traditional dance and traditional healer hierarchy. Our beads and clothes are like the badges that nursing sisters wear. Today I am very proud to be a full-fledged sangoma, to have finally turned to my true calling. It is not in conflict with my Catholic upbringing because I believe in God and the ancestors, who are just like the guardian angels who go between ourselves and a busy God. It hurts me to see church people being hypocritical about traditional healing. Many church-going people say they don't go to traditional healers, but at night they queue up outside my house. It does not need to be this way, so hidden. The two can be combined openly and with honour.

'During training and even today, I learn much about the herbs through dreams. For instance, a person will bring me herbs that I am not familiar with. I keep those herbs because I know I will eventually dream what they are, how they are to be used and even what patient the herbs are for. In my tradition, I don't throw bones. I simply pray for guidance from the ancestors and guardian angels and I am told, in detail, exactly what to do. My Gran brought me to healing and is still my most active ancestor and advisor today. She is often the one showing me the new herbs and their use in treatments.

'As a sangoma, I have to really thank the ancestors who guide me – but even an ordinary person can learn from their advice. Our ancestors speak to each of us in many ways. They may try to reach us through a dream or a vision. They may speak to us as a voice in our head that suggests an idea. Their help is always available. We just have to be quiet to hear and be willing and ready to take their direction.

'We need more cooperation between doctors and healers in Africa. We each have our specialities, our strengths and our weaknesses. It is high time to stop saying "I can" to a patient when I know I cannot. We must refer to other traditional healers or to doctors. To make a better life, we should not judge or assume, and not punish in revenge. God and the ancestors are there to judge and punish.

'Traditional healers have good, safe herbal treatments and healers like me know when to refer patients for medical help. We have developed good relationships with medical people in our communities. But more important, we understand the psychological problems of the disease. Say a pregnant patient begins bleeding. This is an emergency. She may lose the baby. I will get her to the nearest hospital. After she is treated though, especially if she loses the baby, a traditional consultation with the ancestors is needed. The patient must know what is the cause of this misfortune. Did she offend her ancestors? Must she perform some traditional ceremonies to put things right again? The medical side cannot help with this. This is our speciality.

'We are seeing such a breakdown of our natural, traditional order in South Africa. In the cities – especially Johannesburg, Durban, even here in 'Maritzberg, people don't follow the old rules. Because of this we see confusion, violence, crime, even abuse to our own families. There is no order, no traditional rules to follow in these modern places. We need herbs and treatments, ceremonies and contact with the ancestors to keep marriages strong, to keep families strong, to raise our children properly.

'There are many good doctors and nurses who understand that their patients see us traditional healers first and last. These medical people are really working with us, but they are too few. Dr Roz Coleman worked with the Amatikulu Training Centre to improve the relations between healers and doctors on primary health care. Government clinics like Inanda refer their HIV patients to traditional healers. Patients who test HIV positive are told by medical doctors that they have an incurable disease. Well, in our Zulu culture, "an incurable disease" can only be treated by a traditional healer. The traditional healers come to us at ATICC and we go to them with training workshops because they need to, and want to, understand and stop this terrible disease. They are seeing it grow too fast.

'Sometimes it is a struggle to get the hospitals to give counselling to HIV/Aids patients. The hospital staff may be overworked, seeing too many patients, but even so, we hear of an insensitivity toward persons with HIV/Aids. Medical staff don't always see the need for pre-test counselling. There are Aids wards in the Durban hospitals but no counselling staff are posted as part of the normal health team. Aids counselling is an extra duty taking them away from their other responsibilities. You can see the problems with this. A traditional healer also may be very overworked but she has this higher calling. She has a bigger boss to answer to. She will try very hard to counsel and serve that person with HIV/Aids, their family and even their whole community. She will understand and never judge that person. It is not surprising that medical people are referring their patients to us, is it? But this partnership must become stronger, and it will.'

Queen Ntuli –
Zulu healer at South Africa's
first traditional hospital

reedom Traditional Hospital is the first of its kind in South Africa. It is here that traditional healer Queen Ntuli treats patients and trains health workers. Like Isaac Mayeng and Nomsa Dlamini, Queen is a person of both science and tradition. She throws bones to diagnose but in addition may also check her 'answers from the ancestors' with a blood pressure machine and thermometer, or send blood and fluid samples for analysis to the medical facilities with which she cooperates. Only natural herbs are used in the traditional treatments at the hospital. Her plants, roots and bark are specially collected throughout South Africa and beyond, then prepared for her in a laboratory using only natural and pure manufacturing processes, on Warwick Avenue in Durban.

This unique traditional hospital sits in the middle of Durban's busy central business district, near a labourers' hostel and close to government hospitals and clinics. Dr Kwadi, a medical doctor practising nearby at his Field Street clinic, and Queen frequently refer patients to each other. Queen believes that some diseases are better treated by traditional

African methods, while others respond best to western procedures. For instance, western medicine is seen as best for emergency and critical care and Queen has ambulance service on twenty-four hour call for these cases. For many, it is often a combination of treatments and therapies that serves the patient best. As Queen says, 'People have placed their faith in traditional healing for generations, yet they hear of miracles of modern science. We try to offer them both, the best of both worlds.'

I was impressed with how clean, orderly and friendly Freedom Traditional Hospital was on my visit. Queen herself smiled easily, in spite of her heavy work load. She seemed to brighten every room she walked into. The laughter and smiles, the all-around good naturedness of the staff and the patients was something I hadn't seen in a health facility this size. The place was bustling with activity, yet everyone seemed to know their responsibility and specific job. Jars of herbs and bark were being labelled and organised along one wall. Patient records were being updated and examined by the nurses. It was like being inside a well-oiled machine. There was much consulting and conferring going back and forth and a wonderful passion for learning. It was a fun place to be.

'My parents did not believe in traditional healing ways. My father was a reverend in the Methodist Church, which forbade visits to the healers, but when I became so ill with the sangoma sickness, they found the medical side could do nothing. They tried the hospitals, then the faith healers of the Apostolic Church. Finally, they had no choice but to consult the traditional side. This traditional healing was a new world to them, a world they didn't trust.

'I was born on 13 October 1959 in KwaMgwanase in KwaZulu Natal, near Mozambique. My parents moved to Durban when I was a child and I schooled there, through high school and matric. While in school, I began having trouble with my eyes and with headaches so severe I would become unconscious. I was bleeding frequently and unexpectedly. There was no relief from my discomfort. It was a frightening and worrying time.

'My illness continued through teacher training college, as I taught school, and even later into my secretarial course at the Merebank Technikon. The headaches became worse. I couldn't eat. My sleep was disturbed by bad dreams. Finally I did visit a traditional healer who threw bones and mixed a special herbal medicine or muti for me. That evening my headaches stopped and sleep came nicely. My ancestors visited me then and told me I must study to become a sangoma.

'I immediately felt relief. It was like a miracle, to have such pain removed instantly. I felt, finally, here is someone who can help me. Instead of returning to my studies, I went back to this traditional healer. He invited me to study at his home in the Nimfume Royal Areas on the South Coast. The ancestors confirmed this was the proper place for me through my dreams. So, in 1983 I trained for one year. The old lady who trained me was a sangoma and a Reverend in the Zionist church. She used herbs and faith healing. During the training I learned all about herbs, how to diagnose and cure illness, how and when to look into the future to help patients. The ancestors continued to come to me in my dreams and taught me much more, including the ethics of healing. My ancestors have a high morality and told me I must also.

'After training, in 1984, the ancestors told me I must begin my healing practice in Durban, where I was also to take on students of my own. For the first time in my adult life I felt happy in my work. I was using all I had learned in my teacher training course and combining it with this new wonderful healing knowledge. I was so happy to share all I had learned with these students who found their way to me, just as I had "found" my teacher.

'My mother, a trained midwife, was a big help to me with my healing practice. She worked on the medical side and I on the traditional. Our patients could benefit from both. So, you see, my cooperation with the medical world started right at the beginning of my healing practice. Early on I also joined the Sunshine Traditional Healers Association and began studying a wider range of medicines, homeopathy and western health science. In the Sunshine Healers Association I met DrTS Kwadi, a man who has had a big influence on my life. We cooperate and consult together on clients even today. He taught me about Aids and showed me how to further combine modern and traditional medicine.

'I am a sangoma and a faith healer. This works out well because there are some patients who don't believe in herbs so I have to pray for them, for their troubles. I will spend three to seven days praying for their problems to be solved. The patients will stay with me during this time. In these treatments I use holy water, candles, my Bible. Most of my patients, though, use both praying and herbs. It is the unusual one who only uses prayers or only herbs. Most of the patients mix the two. With my type of calling and background, I know how and when to mix these things. Today, with my traditional healing, faith healing and home-Ñopathy, there are few patients I cannot find a way to help. In addition,

I also consult with and learn from a medical doctor who has a surgery in my house. Some of my patients need the herbs and the faith healing, but some are so ill they need the emergency care of a doctor. That is why I asked this colleague to come practise from my home.

'I stay at Follweni Township where there are no services and there is no government or private doctor, no clinic, no hospital. People are suffering when they come to my house and I must call an ambulance. Otherwise people have to walk to the police station and ring the ambulance from there. Very, very ill people can even die while they are waiting a long time for all of this. This area, Follweni, has had many riots, burning of houses and much unrest. People who wanted to come in and help us were afraid. It was not a safe place. For the moment it is more quiet and a clinic is being built. It was not my idea, but the community's idea that the new government clinic be located next to me and I am pleased.

'After my training in November 1983 I returned home and was introduced to the community as a sangoma. I had the usual ceremony. I slaughtered the goat and then the cow. I had to find the hidden things. I had to demonstrate to my community that I really was a sangoma. Immediately after this ceremony, patients started coming to me. I noticed that if the patient has a headache, I will feel it in my head. The information about the person and the illness comes very quickly. In moments I know why they have the pain, where the pain is, and how to heal it.

'In places like Swaziland, especially the rural areas, it is the tradition to really believe in the throwing of bones. The patients expect this. If the sangoma does not throw bones, the patient can be very uncomfortable and not have faith in the healer or the healing. However, the sangoma may not need to throw bones to get the information. It just comes directly to them from the ancestors as well. Out of respect for the patient, to keep them comfortable he or she will throw bones – but before those bones even hit the mat, already the healer knows what is what.'

I n July 1996 we started the Freedom Traditional Hospital. We began with a small clinic for patients and we taught groups of student nurses who wanted to learn about the traditional side. The nursing students train for one year with four months of theory before they start their practical. There is much they need to understand about the traditional side of their patients. These nurses found me and applied for this type of training. In order to qualify they must have passed standard ten, have a first aid certificate, and have done home nursing training. If we find their training in these areas is weak, I give a refresher course with my medical colleague Dr Kwadi.

'The fee for the nurse training is R400 per student. It does not cover our costs but is some small contribution. We accommodate up to fifty nurses at a time. For the most part, the nurses will stay with us and continue to work in this type of traditional hospital. These nurses then will understand the symptoms, know how to treat, know what herbs to prepare – but they are not sangomas. If any of our nurses go on to work in a government hospital or have to liaise with medical doctors, the traditional training will be invaluable. It will offer much-needed information to the attending medical people, who do not understand the traditional side. The national Department of Health has visited my hospital but is unable to give financial support because we are a private hospital. We continue to talk and hopefully over time, they will find the means to help.

'My patients come from all over, from Johannesburg, Cape Town, Zululand. Our reputation is spreading throughout South Africa. When patients come to us, the nurses interview them first. Some respond well to that and the nurses can do some preliminary information gathering for me and for their records. Some of the patients do not want to answer questions and must see me first. In the tradition of the sangoma, I must tell them what is wrong, what is happening. Only then do they know I am a good sangoma. They can be helped by the nurses once that contact is made. I must see each and every patient. From July to October 1996, I saw about a thousand patients.

'Traditional healer Mntshali works with me here. He has such a love and a big gift for this healing work. You can see what a great favourite of the staff and our patients he is. He's been deaf since the age of twelve so he has an assistant write down everything the patient may say during a consultation. He carries an exercise book and pen, which he uses too. The only time he is really confident speaking, rather than writing, is when he is getting messages from his ancestors. In that moment when he is speaking, when he is consulting, he is very clear.

'I could not possibly do this work on my own, as we see patients round the clock. We refer some patients straight to the King Edward or other hospitals. If a patient comes in very dehydrated, we cannot treat him with herbs. He must go to the hospital immediately. Some patients are asthmatic and need critical attention only a hospital can give. Some are seriously injured and need the hospital's emergency care. The patients who need HIV/Aids testing must go to the hospitals and clinics. We then need to see the results of the tests. We are using safe practices such as using surgical gloves, sterilised razors used only once then thrown away, this type of thing, to protect ourselves and our patients from spreading the virus any further.

'Our standards are high, our records are detailed and well kept, our hygienic procedures are strictly followed. Herbal mixtures are well stored and labelled, with dosages explained. I find that in addition to my sangoma training, my homeopathic studies are also helpful in establishing and managing these high operating standards.

'Many people are told to come to us by their medical staff. They are not referred properly in writing because the government has no policy yet about traditional healing and cooperation with a facility such as ours. However, the referral process is already happening, such as the TB cases coming in with a note from their doctors advising me about the tablets they are taking. Eventually I hope to be freer to advise others all over the country. Many have asked us to help them establish this type of hospital in their communities. For now, we are struggling with our own expenses. We do not even own a car. So many people are coming from afar. We must teach others so they can establish their own facilities. We must teach the future teachers who will work with these nurses, for instance. The need, the interest, the demand, are too, too great.

'What is my speciality? I am a general practitioner. I treat conditions such as stroke, diabetes, asthma, personal and emotional problems, trouble at work, bad luck in relationships, marriage, and many others. We advise on various problems. Some patients have been certified as mad by the mental hospitals, yet they may only need to have the bad spirits chased away. It is often just a traditional illness that the western medical doctors cannot treat, so they label them mentally ill, incompetent. These patients often find their way to us and we have been able to help.

'One woman brought her domestic worker to me. This worker had been diagnosed with hysteria. Through traditional means, I cured her of this hysteria and today she is back to work and so happy. Some patients come in unable to speak or carry on normal conversations, making only animal sounds. These I have cured as well. I have also successfully treated cases of epileptic seizures, cases of nightmares, suicidal patients, infertility, unemployment, personal and economic misfortunes.

'We in South Africa have experienced so much trauma. The healers are needed now more than ever. In the case of sexual and child abuse, we are counselling the entire family. Now there are increasing incidents of sexual abuse of children, continued violence and high crime rates. These abusers and criminals have lost their traditions, their customs. That is why they can even consider sexually abusing their own daughters. Something has gone terribly wrong there. Disturbed people such as these who are committing such acts, need a big return to their customs and to the natural laws of life and man.

'We also see a lot of asthma and diabetes. Some of these patients are breathing in waste material coming from the factories where they stay. Chemicals being released, serious air pollution is affecting many people. Diabetes in some patients is partly a result of poor diets. We use a detoxification programme with such patients. We do make use of enemas, emetics and other purification procedures as necessary. We teach them to eat nutritious foods. In western countries, people are living longer. They are exercising regularly, they are eating more natural foods. They are learning how to live better. This sedate life, sitting around, riding taxis everywhere, it is not a natural life. We used to walk in our day-to-day life and eat only what we grew. It is all changed now and we haven't completely adjusted to this urban living. Many illnesses come of this lack of proper adjustment to life in the city.

'I see my patients' symptoms begin to disappear over time. I see this even in HIV/Aids patients, but I cannot say I have a cure for anything because we don't have a proper testing facility. However, we seem to be prolonging and improving the quality of their lives through diet, herbal treatments and exercise. The time they have remaining can be a better life, the people can be more productive. The biggest thing we give our HIV patients is hope. We counsel our HIV patients and suggest modifications in their lifestyles. We supply the clients with condoms.

'Some people show no signs of HIV. Perhaps they have had blood testing done for insurance reasons and the results come back: "You are HIV positive." They become very, very frightened. They believe they will die soon, their days are numbered. They can't even eat and take proper care of themselves because of this worry. They are not happy, thinking about this day and night, they lose weight. The staff at testing facilities, clinics and hospitals must find a better way of telling the patients, counselling the patients. There needs to be pre- and post-test counselling. The medical staff need to be trained and re-oriented. They must be more sensitive to the patients. So now these patients come to me and I have to undo this bad experience caused at the clinics. I must build back their confidence because this worry and depression can kill.

'Counselling and awareness building are also needed for the family of the patient with HIV and the community in general. Currently many people think this HIV thing is bad and the person who gets it, is a bad person as well. So at a time when the person needs support and understanding the most, they are isolated. The patient wants to keep the results secret and I must help them understand that their partners must also come in for testing. This thing cannot be a secret. I am counselling the family, the communities, and getting good results. Once people understand, they can be very, very helpful to their loved ones.

'For sexually transmitted diseases (STDs), we first send the patient to the medical doctor for antibiotics. This is very important. If they don't take the antibiotics, they will spread the disease. While they are taking antibiotics I treat them with complementary herbs. During the entire course of these treatments, the patient must use condoms. We take no chances that the disease may be spread further. We also counsel patients with STDs. Some come to us thinking that they have been bewitched or their problem is a traditional one. It is not, it is an STD and they must recognise this and take proper action.'

Queen takes *thwasas,* or trainees, who dream of her and are led to her by their ancestors. She trains them in stages, providing practical experience. The length of training depends on the individual's abilities and background knowledge. Queen says that some of the *thwasas,* upon completing training, return to their former professions and careers, never to open a healing practice. The training itself brought back some balance to their lives and removed the pain and discomfort they might have been experiencing. In these instances, the training was the treatment.

Queen sees improved and holistic health care developing in South Africa. She is busy training a new type of healer to function in an integrated system where a patient can expect coordination and perhaps a combination of traditional and western medical treatments, depending on their diagnosis. Queen is preparing for the future taking her guidance from her ancestors and medical colleagues alike, but in the meantime, hundreds of patients find their way to her door and the good work, both ancient and modern, continues.

Mercy Manci –
Xhosa healer and founder of
Nyangazezizwe Traditional Doctors
Organisation

ercy Manci, an accomplished Xhosa healer, is well respected in the traditional healing community. She has presented her work in Japan, Germany, Jamaica, the United States and several African countries. Nyangazezizwe Traditional Doctors Organisation was founded by Mercy in 1989 to bring traditional healers together to address professional concerns, and to share information and training programmes. Headquartered in Gauteng Province, Nyangazezizwe currently has 4Ä585 members (all practising traditional healers) from five regions of South Africa.

Nyangazezizwe recognises the importance of achieving financial independence for itself as an organisation, and for the communities it serves across South Africa. It has created self-help projects that include a sewing school where community students graduate every three months, able to produce a variety of goods (dresses, duvets, sheets, etc.), and bakery, brick-making and candle-making projects. Adult literacy schemes, typing and computer skills are also taught. Since traditional healers are the first point of contact on health issues for most of the rural population, Nyangazezizwe believes that literate traditional healers can play a critical role in documenting and providing data to the national health leadership for consideration in health policies and planning. Nyangazezizwe also lobbies government on the issue of statutory recognition for traditional healers.

International donors supported Nyangazezizwe's efforts to unite the leadership of traditional healers on HIV/Aids issues through the funding of a variety of training workshops, meetings and World Aids Day activities between 1994 and 1996. Unfortunately, the coordinating council of 36 leaders of traditional healers was short-lived. Like many efforts before and since, the exercise deteriorates when the traditional healer leadership vies for authority and position. However, if there ever was an issue that could unite the traditional healers' efforts, it is said to be the Aids epidemic. Even so, formal structures such as the one Nyangazezizwe went to great lengths to foster, seem to fail. A neutral body that cuts across traditional healer organisations, sponsored perhaps by government or a neutral third party, may succeed where other attempts have failed. It is also felt by many that until the traditional healers themselves can organise into a professional body, no amount of outside coercion will help.

Formal structures aside, there is every evidence of traditional healers cooperating freely with each other and with the medical community when it comes to their practices and patients. Healing becomes the focus and politics are readily put aside. Nyangazezizwe is an excellent example of this. Contracted to implement an HIV/Aids training programme for healers, Nyangazezizwe recruited leaders from traditional healer organisations across eight regions of South Africa. These traditional healers had no problems training together.

Nyangazezizwe Traditional Doctors Organisation began in Mercy's rural village of Hlwahlwazi in 1989. An office in the nearby town of Flagstaff, an hour's drive away on a dirt road, became a necessity for the group's increasing administrative work, which could not be supported due to the lack of services in the rural areas.

On my visit to the Transkei, I was heartily welcomed by the Nyangazezizwe Flagstaff and Hlwahlwazi branch manager, Mary Nomnqua, and a group of excited traditional healers. Aids posters depicting preventive measures were displayed throughout the office. Computer and photocopy machines, donated by the Sorghum Beer Company, were in use. The space was well organised and clean. Six traditional healers aged thirty-five to fifty, each with a minimum of ten years' experience with practices in Hlwahlwazi, Bizana, Thabankulu, Lusikisiki, Kokstad and Flagstaff, visited with me. Though they had travelled some distance to meet, they were very energetic and excited to share their experience and thoughts.

HIV/Aids was foremost in their minds, both the increasing numbers of infected patients they are seeing and their own alarm at the lack of resources available to them to fight this deadly disease. Each of these rural healers had attended training on HIV/Aids and had since incorporated this new knowledge into their standard course of training for sangoma initiates. These impressive traditional healers and their other colleagues in Nyangazezizwe further maximise the Aids and other primary health care training by making use of 'CeCe' gatherings. CeCe, a large gathering of traditional healers for the purpose of re-introducing a recently graduated healer initiate to his or her community, can be attended by hundreds of traditional healers from the region. Nyangazezizwe traditional healers provide workshops, demonstrations and refresher lectures at these gatherings. They also share any new national and international information they may have received from their headquarters in Gauteng.

Initially they all had difficulties discussing sexuality with each other and with patients. With time, experience and the HIV/Aids training, they have made great strides in overcoming this awkwardness. After learning more about symptoms of sexually transmitted diseases, these Xhosa healers increased the number of referrals they were making to the medical side for lab testing. To avoid spreading infection the healers use a flat, stick-like instrument to apply medicines, such as in the case of an open wound. In this way the healer no longer needs to make contact with the blood. They would much prefer using surgical gloves, to stay in therapeutic touch with their patients, but gloves are expensive and not available in their districts.

The Xhosa healers face other serious constraints. Blood testing is no longer available in Umtata, nor in any other smaller towns or villages in between. Now blood must be sent further away to East London. The tests are too expensive for this rural group. When the healers suspect someone of being HIV positive, 'The patient simply goes home and dies over time. No blood testing is done. When full blown Aids develops, no medication is given to ease the pain and discomfort.' Supplies of all types are in short supply at the government clinics. A senior nursing sister who later joined our discussion and tour of Hlwahlwazi told us that she was constantly obliged to ask the traditional healers for condoms as her supplies often did not arrive. She gave moving testimony to the importance of the Nyangazezizwe healers in the Transkei.

It was impressive how well informed these healers of the Transkei were, given their lack of telephones, radio, television and transport. In addition, many of the healers are illiterate and cannot read what little written material is available. The Nyangazezizwe healers, relying on word of mouth and the use of very simple posters, are making an impact on thousands of people in the communities they serve.

Mercy's story begins like this: 'I was born in the village of Hlwahlwazi in the Eastern Cape of South Africa, about a thirty minute drive from Flagstaff. I was born on 28 September 1955. We are nine children; three girls, six boys. I am the first born. My mother never married and her children had different fathers. My father was a Sotho from Kokstad. Unfortunately he passed away in 1980. My mother is not a sangoma. When I was growing up, my mother's mother was the person who was practising traditional healing, but she married a person who was a Christian reverend. Now in these days, the Christians understood and even consulted the traditional healers, but being the reverend's wife, my Gran could no longer perform these rituals, these healing ceremonies. It was not accepted by the reverend. So she went to a traditional healer for help.

'This healer spoke with her ancestors. The ancestors were not happy. She had been given a gift of healing and was not now using it. The sangoma now slaughtered a black cow to appease the ancestors, to honour them and ask them to please stop asking my grandmother to perform the various ceremonies frowned on by her husband. Now, she still had this healing gift so she continued healing, but without the rituals. She continued to go to the forest, to collect the natural herbs, the medicines. She was quietly helping and healing patients but not charging any fees, because of the church. You see she loved her husband. Out of respect for his work, for his standing in the community, she closed that door to the ancestors. It was very, very difficult for her but her husband was a big person in the community, in an important position. She made this sacrifice out of respect and love for her husband.

'Her ancestors understood her situation and because she made such efforts to communicate with them, they supported her choice. They knew it was difficult to give up her traditional way of life, to no longer perform the healing ceremonies, to leave behind the dancing and drumming of healing. They saw what strength of conviction she had. So, they chose another to perform her duties and let her continue healing in her own quiet way. The ancestors remained close to her. This is how it is with ancestors, perhaps they ask you to do something that is extremely difficult in your situation or may even offend your loved ones – then you must speak with the ancestors, communicate your struggle with them.

'The ancestors do not desert you simply because you cannot bear their request. They can see if your intent is sincere and honest and they can make a compromise, they can respect your situation. Now, even after my Gran's decision to leave behind these certain ceremonies and outward signs of traditional healing, she continued to 'see' and know things about people. So the community continued to seek her out for help with healing. If the ancestors had been angry or disgusted with her or considered her weak or wrong, then this special ability would have vanished.

'My Gran did not throw bones for diagnosing. The traditional healers in South Africa diagnose in different ways. Some throw bones, some go into a type of trance and the ancestors simply speak through them directly to the patient, some receive information through prayer, it all depends on the gift and particular training of the individual healer. My Gran was one of these types who went into a trance and spoke to the patient, but now it is not my Gran speaking but the ancestors. After the consultation, the patient would see that everything she said was true.

'You see, with the ancestors, we must communicate with them, because we are not living in the place of the ancestors. We are living here, among man. So we must explain and talk to the ancestors, help them understand our world as well. So even if I throw bones and I say this and that about the bones, it is really the ancestors who are speaking through me. I am their messenger, I deliver their words. But whether it is a healer who goes into a trance and cannot be disturbed while the ancestors are speaking through her or, like myself, someone who throws bones, at some point the ancestors stop speaking, full stop. It is then that the patients may speak and tell the healer anything that they are feeling or are concerned about in what the ancestors just said. So always, it is a two-way communication. The patient must respond and say, "Yes, I know it is like that" or "Yes, I agree with what you say" or "Yes, but I am also worried about this pain, or this relationship, or this something else in my life." Always the sangoma, the healer, must give the patient a quiet moment, a time to respond to the news from the ancestors. All good African traditional healers will practise this way.'

'To help a patient, that is foremost in my mind, always,' says Mercy. 'I don't worry about receiving payment, that will come as the ancestors see fit. Some traditional healers become more concerned about what the patient can pay them, "Is this illness something that will require many treatments and herbs, so I will earn a good fee?" It is the wrong way around to practise. The patient comes first, the healing is first, a healer cannot concentrate on how much money they need to make. This way of looking at a patient and healing can confuse and even ruin a healer. It is not proper. The healing gift is from God and the ancestors. It is up to them to show us the way and provide for us. The ancestors are very clever and they will look after us if we treat this healing gift with great respect and humbleness.

'Once I asked my mother, "Why do other healers point a finger at me, why do they sometimes treat me cruelly? I seem to look different to the healers. I must be wrong somehow." Then my mother explained. At birth I was covered by a white substance, a "net" my mother called it. Other people are simply born without this, but I was covered. This is unusual. When my mother saw me like this, my Gran and she knew immediately that this was a special child, a gift from God. This child some day will be a leader. They didn't know at that time that I would be a healer, they only believed that this child is a lucky person. To be born this way, she has special protection.

'As a child growing up I could feel that I was set apart. I could especially feel this when my grandmother was alive, because my mother used to work. She was a domestic worker in Durban. She used to leave her children with her mother. So my brothers and sisters, we all grew up with my Gran. That Gran taught me to take responsibility. The water had to be fetched by me, our food was cooked and served by me. I had to be sure there was enough water for everyone to wash before they went to school, that there was enough wood for cooking, that the pots were clean for cooking, that the mealies were ground for the soft porridge I made each morning, that the cow dung was collected for cleaning the floors.

'I had to come home early from school and look after the family. If there was a guest, I had to prepare tea. I also had to see that my Gran had enough snuff. It was me who used to grind her snuff. That grinding stone was so big. She taught me, sitting next to her; she showed me how to take it and grind and make the snuff just so. When I was finished, I carried this big heavy grinding stone back – but it was too heavy and I couldn't hold it – it dropped and crushed my toes. At times like that, this "gift" that made me special seemed like a punishment to me. I used to wonder, Why me, having to do all this work, why me? A young person like me, it was a big, big responsibility. I couldn't understand.

'Now that I am leading other healers I can understand completely, that this was good training for me, though it was a very, very painful way of life. There are other ways to provide this training to a child without being so harsh. Today I think you can sit down with a child and speak with them, help them bit by bit to understand the situation, how they are special, how they must prepare to accept this calling, this specialness. A child can learn and accept without such a severe life, I believe.

'I was attending school and carrying this great responsibility and our money was short. I couldn't afford uniforms or shoes. Also at school, just like at home, the teachers selected me to be responsible for the other students in my class. I was always the prefect. I had to see that students arrived on time, did their homework properly, cleaned the classroom. There must be no noise in the classroom. Any problem in these areas (and there were many), then I would be called to the principal to answer.

'It was a tough time. I had big responsibilities at home, at school, and I was involved in agriculture. I had to see that the plants were grown properly because that was our food. The work at secondary school was too great and the responsibilities at home were even greater. I was so tired by the end of the day. I had no time, no time to play with my friends, my life was only work. So in Form III, when I was eighteen years old, I stopped. This was 1974, and I came home.

'At home I concentrated on church. But at church it was the very same thing! I belonged to the Roman Catholic Church. I joined the 'Cross of Jesus', a society for mature women. We wore a red ribbon to show we belonged to this special group. It was a happy thing, a happy time. This was a preparation for the sisterhood. If I had continued with this training, I would have become a nun. We were like novices. We were trained and our commitment and conviction were tested. We were being prepared for a celibate life, devoted to Jesus. We would be married to Jesus serving the Roman Catholic church.

'Now even there, they gave me the responsibility for our group. One of our duties was to visit the sick people and pray for them. We would pray the rosary. I would pray to God, "This person is yours. This person is in great pain. Please I appeal to you, rescue this person from the suffering by either healing him or taking him from this earth." Some patients were so ill they were not able to talk. They were not eating. They were withering away in their bodies. Somehow, after I prayed for them, there was a difference. They would open their eyes, look at me, look at the others, speak and ask for water and just become well. The other women and the patients noticed this phenomenon. So each time they urged me to please accompany them.'

ater I was grabbed, yes, I will call it grabbed, by another family. I was in the village, in a poor rural area. If a family wanted to marry you but had no money, had no 20 cows for lobola (the bride price), they could just steal you away. For some time such a family had wanted me for their son. One evening I was washing at the river. Men came at the river and they grabbed my arms. I fought and fought but they were stronger. I recognised these men, one was my mother's neighbour, still young, my age. The two men took me to a house and one of the men left. Now I understood they want me for this man. They locked the door to the house. I could not get out.

'Much, much later he came to talk with me. I wanted nothing to do with him. He brought me a bowl of soup. I didn't take it. I wanted nothing from this man. Later still he came back and just took off my clothes. I was alone. There was no one to help me, to stop him. I had no choice. He jumped on me, he shook, shook me. I was a virgin at this time.

'The next day I couldn't go home even if I had had the choice because now I am no longer a girl, a virgin. So I stayed with this man. The very next day we went to tell my grandmother. My Gran had no idea that this was going to happen to me. However there had been a sign of sorts. This family lived next door to my grandmother. They had moved to this house with their son, but it was not their normal house. He and his family were from Ciskei, not Transkei. It was unusual that they should have stayed there. We should have suspected something about these people. It was not right.

'My grandmother charged this family seven cows for me, but they could only pay four. I stayed with this man's family but later they moved back to Ciskei. They took me with them. This man who took me was old. If he had been younger and a virgin, he would have approached my family and proposed marriage in a proper way. He was greedy or anxious, too eager to have me in his family. He had been watching me, observing me, wanting me for a long time. Also he knew I was a church person who could not marry him this way. He knew in the church, you "must go through the door, not sneak through the window" to marriage. In the proper church way, he knew this road to marriage would be very long. He did not want to wait.

'So it was there, in the Ciskei, that my daughter was born. Later I discovered that my husband would leave me at the homestead with his family and go to other women. There was no proper wedding really, only a traditional wedding ceremony. In the eyes of my ancestors, this family was saying we are married. This marriage was not a good thing. How can a man marry a person, and leave her to go to other women? This man took me while I was a virgin! So this means he is planning to divorce me. Aha, I begin to see by his behaviour what is his plan. So I say to myself, let me not have any more children. Let me study further and complete my education. I used to dream about being a nurse at times. I decided to pursue this and wrote to Damelin College at Lady Frere in Ciskei while I lived in Mhlalga village. I could study by correspondence.

'My husband started work in the mines. In January, he would leave for the whole year. He would send money which at that time was enough. In December he would come back home. Even though he would see me only one time a year, he would still leave me to go to other women during his visit. I worried that he might divorce me before I can finish my goal of nursing. So let me do something where I can support myself when this thing happens. I decided I must not become a domestic worker. Rather let me do something that will put me in the office, secretarial worker or something like that.

'Damelin sent me books and I bought a typewriter. I used to close my door and teach myself and practise. I also went to the clinic and asked for birth control tablets. You cannot, in our tradition, take any such tablets. You are not allowed to ask for such things at the clinic. The man married you to bear children and you must. That is it. I looked for a clinic and asked for the sister in charge. I took a chance explaining my situation to that sister. I was very honest and I told her, this marriage will come to an end, I can see this. So when this marriage comes to an end, I do not want to have a lot of kids. Well, this sister could see it too. With one child, I was able to keep my daughter with me and care for her, but if I had more children, it would not be so easy. So the sister gave me the tablets and I kept studying.

'Later my husband came. You see, in this family I took responsibility again. I worked for his family, fetched water, did everything just like when I was at home. But as I started to be busy with my studies, learning how to type, his family became jealous. When my husband visited, they told him, "Ah, she doesn't have time, she changed and there is something wrong with her. She is always busy with books and typing. She has no time for us." He was so angry, he took all my books and burned them in a big fire, he broke, he kicked, he smashed the typewriter into pieces. I said to him, "You can burn the books but the whole information is here, in my mind." I was so angry – but I stopped studying.'

'Later, he took me to the traditional healers because he wanted to know what was wrong. My daughter was growing up, she was four years old, but I was not getting another child. I used to despise healers. Because of church, I stayed away from these healers. I didn't like the ceremonies, dancing, drumming, wearing traditional clothing, wearing smelly skins and things like that. When I used to see these healers as a child, I would even shout rude things to them. I didn't understand at all.

'My husband took me to several traditional healers. One was a woman in Aliwal North, far, far away from where we stayed. The woman said, "Okay, you tell me about the problems." So, I knew now this was not a sangoma because you had to tell her your problems! She should have known through the ancestors what was wrong. So the family told her I wasn't getting pregnant, was I bewitched or what? They didn't know.

'The healer claimed she would take out whatever I was bewitched with. She went to her place and came back with a bowl and razors. She said I must kneel and take off my clothes. I was so angry to have to take off my clothes. She cut me in three places, it was so painful. Then she started to suck the blood from me and it was painful. She didn't put in any herbs, just started sucking hard and even biting me. I complained but she shouted at me. I just kept quiet.

'I knew there was nothing wrong with me, there was nothing she could "take out". Then she shouted, "Something is coming out!" Nothing came out from my body, but in the bowl was the skin of a snake. She took this snake skin from her mouth, from her mouth to the bowl. It was a trick. Then again she sucked hard on these cuts on my body and out she spit some brown hair. Again she sucked and spat something like meat from her mouth. She told the family to come near and see these things. She had tricked them. I could even see as she was treating me, these things were not coming from my body but only from her mouth.

'She showed the family and said I was bewitched by these things. The snake prevented me from getting pregnant, the hair was pubic hair from a corpse, a dead person, and the small piece of meat was from a placenta. At this point the healer went outside to bury these things. I also asked to go outside and get some air. When I went out I saw her. She was pretending to dig as if she was burying something. After she returned to the house, I went behind to look at this place. There were only scratches, she buried nothing. She was keeping these things and using them to trick other patients. I knew she was tricking us but I also knew some day we would get her.

'She charged the family R800. This was an expensive treatment. She said I must stay with her for one week so she could continue to treat me. The family was to return in one week to collect me. I was so happy. Now I could observe her and catch her in her tricks.

'The following day a man came to her in terrible pain. I noticed that this woman, this so-called healer, always sat next to the door so she could see if someone was coming. Then she could jump up and prepare whatever she needed to trick these people. I watched her very carefully. Finally, I caught her as she pretended to eat something, then put these objects in her mouth to use against the patient. When the family came, this woman said she would return with us to look after me and see how everything was in our house. I was so glad to hear her say this. Now I would expose her when she was up to her tricks at my home. I knew I would really catch her now.

'When she came to treat me at home, many people came to watch her. This woman was going to charge the family again. It was so wrong. Such a cheat. I told my husband that this woman was a fraud. He did not believe me. He said, "There is something wrong with you and now, finally, you will be helped." So, the neighbours came, lots of people came. She would always work from behind a blanket, hiding herself from those watching her. I would follow her later and see where she "buried" the things she had "sucked" out but, of course, there was no hole, there was nothing buried.

'Finally her last day came and I had not caught her out yet. I would go in her room when she was out and look inside her medicine bag. I found none of the things she used to trick. On this last day, I gave her water and tea in the morning. She drank tea, she ate breakfast and bathed. Later she went to the toilet outdoors. I ran to her bag. Something said to me, "Look under the chair." I looked and there was a bag, a pouch that used to hold Horseshoe brand chewing tobacco. This pouch was very dirty and seemed full of things. I looked inside, it was full of all these things, snakes, hair, all the things she was using. I took it but I wasn't sure how I was going to use it.

'I quickly went to my husband's father's brother's house. I showed them, "You see – it is as I have been telling you. All she does is a fraud."

'They said, "Quick, take it back to her."'

'I walked back and began to prepare our meal. The woman returned to her room and later came to eat with us. She was now very, very upset. She could not even talk. She was looking, looking for something. People were coming around. They wanted to see her perform this special sucking treatment.

'She said, "No, I cannot work now. I don't feel well, this weather is not right for me." People were begging her for this treatment, but no, she said she could not.

'The time came for us to take her to the station so she could catch her train and return home. Something came into my head, saying: "You have seen her dirty work, so now why do you keep her things? This is how she has survived all these years, doing this dirty work. Give her back her things." I thought, "Oh no, how can I give it to her now?" So, as she was preparing to leave, I simply put the bag on the floor where I knew she must pass.

'She was out near the gate, walking very slowly. I stood next to my bag and shouted, "What is this?"

'My husband said, "No, that is rubbish. Throw it out."

'"No!" she screamed, and flew across to us. She grabbed the bag and put it inside her things. She said she would come next time and treat all the others, but she never returned, because we knew her tricks.'

I never did get pregnant. My sister-in-law knew I was taking birth control tablets. Finally she told my husband. He was so angry and again remembered the books, the typewriter. He told me to go, as I had never finished being a girl and was not prepared to be a real wife and have his children.

'I said, "If you really want that, you just write a letter saying that to my family, because it was you who took me in the first place. You must release me from marriage."

'He wrote and posted the letter but before a response came from my Gran, he took me to the train station.

'I felt a pain, a deep sadness. I was not a girl any more because he spoiled my virginity. Where did I fall? I was not a girl, but I was no longer a wife. I was just a second-hand person. I could not go home. There was no place for me there if I was no longer a girl. When I was grabbed and violated, I became pregnant immediately, in 1974. My baby was born in August 1975. I left my daughter behind with my husband's family. I told my husband that when he took me I was a virgin but now I've got a child with this family, I must go without her. She was five years old. I wrote a letter to my mother explaining I was no longer a wife and went straight to Johannesburg. It was 1989.'

'I stayed with my mother's brother in the Mofolo North section of Soweto and tried to find work. It was difficult at that time because I didn't have an ID. I was born in the Transkei, a homeland inside South Africa. We had no proper ID, no proper pass required in South Africa. My uncle heard of a doctor who needed an assistant nurse. This doctor was on Wanderers Street, the very same neighbourhood I am in today, in downtown Johannesburg. The doctor, a black man working with a Muslim, hired me. I made the appointments, took payments from the patients and kept patient records. Later the doctor wanted me to give actual treatments to the patients. He would show me the medicines and say, 'You steam this person, you bath this person,' everything like that. He was using some African traditional medicine.

'I was happy to steam or bath a person but I didn't like the way the doctor was diagnosing. To diagnose, he would ask me to boil plain water, put it in a bowl and bring it to him. Next, he would take a plain piece of white paper and ask me to leave the room. While he was alone with the patient, he would pour water on the paper and names would appear. I used to ask the patient, "How did he do this?" Some patients said this was a bad thing. Sometimes patients would be so upset and sad because the doctor had told them they were going to die. This was not right. Of course, it was a trick and he was frightening them.

'The doctor was using a type of invisible ink that is sold as a child's game. He knew by the patient's surname on their file card, what language group they came from. This one was a Xhosa, this one a Sotho, like that. So he would pick up the words he needed to use in their language and write them with this ink that only shows up when the paper upon which it is written is wet. When the patient came, he would say, "Here, take off your shoes and lightly touch this paper with your foot. Now go with Mercy and bathe, prepare for the consultation." Such trickery. I hated to see it. The herbal medicines were true and good remedies and I saw that each preparation was pure. I enjoyed the work with the herbs, very much.

'This medical doctor also diagnosed with a mirror. Now, there are some traditional healers diagnosing with this method in South Africa. Some are tricksters like this doctor, perhaps others are true, I don't

▲ *A healer in the Transkei using materials from the Department of Health in an HIV/Aids workshop.*

▲ *These trainees were led to their teacher Mage Jekeleza (in the headdress with the pink feather) through visions and dreams.*

▼ *Part of a class of healers in training*

▲ *Healer trainees grinding herbs for traditional treatments*

▲ *Me and Mr Sibandze in his muti hat, a warehouse for herbs and traditional medicines*

▲ *In Swazi tradition only traditional healers may wear the ochre in their hair in this particular style.*

▲▶▶ *Khumbulile Mdluli at a healer graduation ceremony.*

▼▶ *Khumbulile Mdluli reading the bones.*

▼ *The Nyangazezizwe Sewing Project in Johannesburg.*

▼ *PH Mntshali - a college educated man who received his 'calling' while working in the private sector.*

▲ *Joubert Dlamini in her traditional pharmacy.*

Negotiating a price at the Mbabane public market, Swaziland.

▲ *Nomsa Dlamini, a healer in the Traditional Medical Practitioners Organisation at her clinic in Soweto.*

Isaac Mayeng, Tswana healer and international researcher in his herbal shop in Guguletu, Cape Town.

▲ *Nomsa Vilakati had no formal training and offered little resistance when she was 'called' to a life of healing.*

know. Perhaps for some good true healers, gifted with this technique, it is possibly an effective way to get information and diagnose. This is how it worked at the doctor's. He gave a mirror to the patient and said, "Go into this room by yourself and just look into the mirror. The image you see in this mirror, this is the person who is bewitching you."

'Once the doctor asked me to accompany a patient into the room. I was curious and asked the patient, "Who do you see in this mirror?"

'He said, "Oh, it is my father's brother who is bewitching me."

'I said, "May I see the mirror, please?"

On the mirror was just a photo. The doctor had cut out many photographs and played tricks with the patient's mind. As the patient quickly glances at the image, aha, he sees someone who just pops into his mind. Perhaps the patient suspects his father is bewitching him and he sees a male image in or on the mirror. Well, one person looks like another and he sees his father. The patient is in an anxious state of mind, is even desperate for help. The doctor exploited this fragile state of mind.

'I looked at the back of the mirror and saw the photo. I showed the patient right then. I said gently, you see this is just a photo. It is not a real thing. Do not worry, do not believe what this man has to say.

'These patients never came back. The doctor was charging as much as R1Ä000 for such treatments. My God, that is so much money for the patients. It was so wrong. There was no higher calling to heal here, not even ordinary ethics.

'I started looking for new work. I quietly asked some of the patients that I could trust, did they know of any good work for me? Remember, I had to look quietly because I had no "dompas", no South African ID, no pass book. I was from the homelands of Ciskei and Transkei. We had no rights to look for work in Johannesburg in those days. One day I met a man who provided security for the building I worked in. I asked him, "Do you know of any jobs? With your company? Maybe with the unions?" At this time it was the unions who were employing black people and were run by black people. I didn't want to work for white people.

'Thanks to my security guard friend's introduction, I was eventually employed by Mr Lekgotlo, at the National Union of Brick and Allied Workers. I worked for him from 1982 to 1983. Sadly, Mr Lekgotlo suffered seriously from asthma problems and was admitted to the hospital. The suffering was so great that he took his own life in the hospital. His position was taken by another man, the General Secretary of the union. It became more and more important that I hold the proper working papers required for black people in South Africa. So unsteady was this situation that I decided to go back home where I was finally able to get a Transkei passport. I returned to Soweto with my new document. It was 1984.'

It was then that the dreams started. In the dreams, I saw myself dancing, being with traditional healers, giving someone a treatment, seeing my patients being healed. I would dream of an old lady, very much like my grandmother, showing me what people were going to come to me and what their problems were. For instance, she might say in the dream, "This woman is coming, she has problems getting pregnant. Here is the medicine you give her, this is how you prepare it." Just like that. She would tell me every detail of what I must do. Then in the dream, the patient would come, I would dig the herb and give the treatment, and the patient would actually be able to become pregnant.

'I couldn't understand this dreaming, so I put it out of my mind during the day. Time passed and I continued to have this problem (because, you see, I thought of the dreams as a problem). I would wake in the morning and go to work. On my way to work I would feel lost. I would suddenly find myself thinking, "Where am I? What is wrong with me?" I would look around and find that I am at the office, working! Sometimes this would happen on the train to work. I wouldn't know where I was coming from. Was I coming from Soweto? I would look out of the window and see – oh, it is facing toward Soweto so I must be coming home from work.

'I would enter the door to my home, my uncle's place, and just sit next to the stove. My uncle would help me by preparing the pots and having the food ready for cooking for me. I would put the meat on the stove, sit down next to the stove and sleep, sleep. He thought I was very tired from working so hard. He would wake me and say, here is food, eat, then go to bed. He also had to wake me for work. It was strange for all of us. I couldn't understand what was happening to me and why – why me? What was the meaning of this illness and the dreams? I used to feel angry. At work they complained that I was sick. I used to wear high-heeled shoes and dress so smartly, but I was losing weight fast. I was disturbed in my mind and it affected my body.

'Later in Soweto I became sick. I began to bleed, but only when I was near a man. This was so peculiar. At the time, I had a boyfriend who was also working at the union. We were not sleeping together. If I was with him, the bleeding would come strong. If I was on the train and the train was very, very full, the men would offer me their seat, and stand so I could rest. But it was no good, for as I stood to leave the train, the seat under me and my clothes would be soaked with blood.

'My boyfriend offered to take me to a traditional healer in Meadowlands. He was so concerned for my health. We did go to the healer, who threw bones. The healer was upset and said, "You insult me. You come for a consultation but the bones show clearly that you are a healer." He gave me some medicine to bathe in. He said, "You are not sick. You are just resisting your calling to become a healer. This call is long overdue. The ancestors have waited too long for you." I took the medicine but I never used it.

'Later I started having pains in the womb. I went to Baragwanath Hospital. They thought there was something in my womb but they didn't know what it was. Dr Mbere, a top gynaecologist, the first black gynaecologist in South Africa, was still working at Baragwanath Hospital. I was taken to the operating theatre but afterwards I went into a coma for three full days. I woke up suddenly from this sleep because someone was talking to me. The doctors and nurses around my bed were shocked that I woke. I was also shocked to find myself in a hospital.

'The nurses and doctors said, "'What happened?"

'I looked at them, they looked at me.

'They repeated, "What happened? What caused you to wake up?"

'I told the doctors I woke up because my grandmother was shouting at me, saying, "Why are you here? Didn't I ask you to take my work? Why you don't want to listen to me? Why are you not taking your call?" She turned, disgusted with me, and began to walk away. I started to call out to her as she was leaving. I wanted to talk with her. It was at this moment that I woke up.

'The doctors said I must rest. Later a nurse came to me and told me I was taken to the theatre – I remembered that – and the doctor opened me but could find nothing. The nurse said she was very sure this was a traditional thing, that I should go to a traditional healer for some help.

'My day came for discharge and I returned to work. I did not go to a healer because I was no longer sick. It was 1985. However, the dreams continued. Now a new thing started happening. After the dreams I would wake and find a medicine in the blankets on my bed. It would be the exact medicine that I had just been dreaming about, the one my grandmother was telling me to use for a certain patient. It happened three times exactly like this. I said to myself, "No, this is impossible. I will simply move to another place." I left Soweto to stay downtown in Johannesburg.

'I continued working for the union. It was my responsibility to resolve grievances brought to the office by our members. I also made appointments for the general secretary, communicated with general management and attended workers' meetings on their work premises. I worked in administration, in accounting, everything. I would go to the bank, make deposits and go to the post office. One day I took all the post to be mailed and the money from the bank withdrawal, and dropped it all into the postbox. I didn't even know I had done that. I returned to the office and continued with my work. Later our driver came for his petrol money. I said, "Money? what money?" He reminded me I had withdrawn money today from the bank. Oh my God, now I remembered what I had done. I immediately rang the postmaster and they were able to stop the mail and they found everything.

'I was getting worried about my condition. After work, I would go home to my room and lock my door. I isolated myself from any social contact outside work, where I had to see people. My boyfriend and others would knock on my door but I would just keep quiet. At night the very same dreams began repeating themselves. I began to wonder, how can this grandmother want me to be a traditional healer? Who will train me? How will it all happen? In Transkei and Natal they put on these smelly skins, that is not for me. In the Transkei when the healers are fortuning, they go into a trance and shout this deep sound from their throats. I do not want to be like them, making these strange sounds. I cannot be trained in Johannesburg. I can't train in this busy city. No, if I am to train it must be a pure place, using pure water and pure life in the rural areas. I must sleep on a natural floor, use only natural light, not electricity.

So, you see, I was beginning to think, slowly, "How can this training happen for me?" It all came very slowly, because I really resisted it. I had a dream where I was on a flat thing, like a bed, on top of the world, and I was flying all over the world. Sometimes I dreamed I was flying from South Africa, crossing a red sea. Why is this, I wondered? Sometimes I dreamed myself flying and my whole body was covered with leopard skins. When I tried to talk in the dream, red flames came out of my mouth. I had whiskers, red eyes and a head like a leopard, but I was a leopard flying, flying over the world.

'Every day now I also had this dream in which I was a healer. I was dancing and being with traditional healers. I would come home from work, lock my door and stay quiet and isolated. One evening in my dream I heard a voice tell me to open the door. I opened the door. There was an old woman, very old, with no teeth, standing at my door. She told me to follow her. I looked around, I thought, "I am not dreaming, I am awake." I was no longer sure when I was dreaming and when I was awake. The dreams were so clear, so like being awake, just the same.

'From 1985 to 1986 these things kept happening. My boss at work said, "Get some help or lose your job." He gave me two weeks to think about it and rest. He said if I needed to go away to look after my health, there would still be a job for me when I came back. I stayed home in my room for the two weeks. I was so worried I couldn't even eat. The dreams continued. Then, on the last night of the two weeks, I dreamed I was in another country, not South Africa. The people of this country wrap fabric around themselves; I was dressed like them. Now in South Africa when people shout 'amandla' they raise their hands one way. In this country when they shout 'amandla', it was different.

'It was 1986 and the singer Letta Mbuli was also in my dream. We listened to her sing but then teargas came and broke up the crowd. Everyone was running to get away from the burning tear gas. I ended up, in the dream, next to some small trees. I was with a woman who was Samora Machel's sister.

'She said to me, "Look at those fighter airplanes in the sky, army planes, brown with red. Those planes come from South Africa to fight Samora Machel."

'I looked up and saw silver army planes coming up from the ground.

'She said, "You see those planes, those silver ones are Samora Machel's planes, fighting the South Africans."

'While we were still looking, the South African plane started to shoot. Bullets were flying all around us. Something told me to look to one side. I looked and I saw Samora Machel's brother and mother on the ground near us. His mother was hit by the bullets from the plane and was struggling with the pain of the bullets. The same voice said to me, "Go and help her, heal her."

'I went to her. She was in great pain. The boy, the brother, was trying to help her but he didn't know what to do.

'Then a voice said to me, "Talk to your ancestors. Ask them what to do.'

'I just knelt down and rubbed the grass and asked them to help me.

Dust was coming out. A bottle appeared and a milky substance was inside. The ancestors said this was a medicine I must give to the mother. I stood up and asked this man to open his mother's mouth. He helped me and we gave her all the medicine. Then all the bullets fell from her body. The man was shocked and the woman, Samora's mother, looked at me and said, "You are the world's healer." I looked over to see the woman I had been sitting with had also been hit by bullets. Helping her was the only thing on my mind. Then, suddenly, I woke up.

'The next morning I returned to work. I told my boss that I must be trained as a traditional healer, that I must be trained outside South Africa, and I must go speak with Samora Machel and tell him about this dream. If I cannot travel out of South Africa because I have no South African passport, only the homeland documents, then I must at least go up to the border of Mozambique, on the Komati side. The name of the place I was to train was Bushbuck Ridge.

'Now my boss said, "Do not tell anyone about this dream, as you will be suspected of trying to hurt Machel. If you speak about it in South Africa, you could be arrested."

'Within two weeks, what I saw in the dream happened. In the papers, I saw that Machel was killed in an airplane which exploded, but the whole story did not come out. The spot where Machel crashed, was exactly the place I saw in my dream. Had I said something about my dream, I would have been identified as an informer.

'I was now dreaming things that were really happening. I had to go and train. This same man drove me to the Komatipoort border. The dreams had shown me a teacher, a toothless lady who was at my door in the dream, but I didn't know yet where she was. My boss could speak Shangaan, the language people spoke in this place. I could not. He asked where this woman healer was. We found one such old woman in Komatipoort, and one in Manyaleti Game Reserve, but neither was the right one from the dream. The next day we started to look again, talking with people, searching far and wide.

'Finally, one man said, "Yes, there is a lady such as you describe." We went with him, and at the door, there she was, exactly like in the dream. I was so completely happy. By then, I had accepted this healing thing. The old woman was also happy to see me, as she had been dreaming about my coming. She told me my ancestor, my grandmother, was a great person, a good person. She wanted everything done properly. I must go home and tell the entire family that I have been called, I have been chosen, and I am accepting it. I must slaughter a goat.

'My family was happy for me. They knew all along that I was chosen. It did not surprise them.

'After my training, in 1988, I was told in a dream that I must open an organisation which would be called after the name given to me in sangoma training, Nyanga Ye Sizwe. My grandmother came to my trainer, the old woman, in a dream and told her this was to be my name. Nyanga Ye Sizwe means "World Healer". The organisation which I formed is called Nyangazezizwe or World Healers. I had a dream that this organisation would be successful in helping the healers of South Africa. We opened first in my home area in the Transkei. I was busy with this and had a busy healing practice as well. I also continued to work at the union offices. In 1990 I started to meet with other traditional healer organisations in Zimbabwe and other places. In 1991 I had to resign from my union job. It was finally time to do my grandmother's work, my healing work, full-time.'

Nhlavana Maseko –
healer to Swazi kings

r Maseko, as he is called by traditional, government and medical leaders alike, is perhaps the most acknowledged and recognised traditional healer in Swaziland. Founder of the Traditional Healers Organisation for Africa (THO) and healer to the current and past Swazi king, he is provocative, dedicated and at times, controversial. There were times when, arriving at the THO in Siteki to collect my interpreter, I would hope that Dr Maseko would not be there. I knew that if he was in I could be delayed by several hours. He was a busy man whose duties required him to travel extensively. When he was back in Swaziland, he had THO business to tend to. That meant initiating and tracking relationships with donors and international funding organisations.

I enjoyed providing the business consulting we had agreed on, but began to feel a strong pressure. My time was short and had to be spent with the healers themselves. I knew I was there for a specific purpose and it was not to expand the THO organisation. That seemed strange, since my professional skills were well suited to the task, but as I became more comfortable in the world of the ancestors and the healers, tending to the business world was often irritating and distracting to me. My mission was not as large as Dr Maseko had originally hoped. That I would not see THO achieve its financial self-sufficiency was a disappointment to him. Dr Maseko's place in my heart grew larger the day he spoke with me about his having to accept my role and my mission. It was not an easy thing for him to discuss with me. Nor was it necessary for someone of his stature to find the time to address this. I will always appreciate that gesture. He cleared the way for me to follow my own calling.

Dr Maseko and the healers I spent time with were highly accomplished and gifted in their healing abilities, but the world of business and physical reality sometimes had them at a disadvantage. This is not so unusual. It's been my experience that a 'gift' or highly developed talent may cause an imbalance in other areas. There is the friend who has a brilliant academic mind but runs out of gas driving to a meeting because she forgot to fill up the car. In the case of the healers, their belief in and strong contact with their ancestors is critical to their manoeuvring the minefields of everyday life. Their sharp intuition guides them eventually to the right resources. They get the help they need, often from a bureaucratic system they don't even understand.

In 1993, Nhlavana Maseko was sixty-three years old and had been practising traditional medicine for thirty-four years. Unlike the other healers I spent time with, Dr Maseko was exposed to life under a great traditional healer, a leader much like himself. Furthermore, he was raised in a traditional manner but ran away to live with a missionary family. It was in this western setting of the church that he received his calling to heal. He tells the story in his own words.

'My grandfather was a gifted traditional healer, a great seer. I grew up at his feet. He was known by all, far and wide. He had many cattle, goats, sheep. He was very powerful. There was a law between the Sotho and the Swazi tribes concerning land. It required my grandfather and others to relocate. We were living in Swaziland at the time but my grandfather decided we would find greener pastures just across the border in the Republic of South Africa. He found a good spot near Witbank. He moved his entire household and cattle. He brought many, many people. He called his place, his community, a word in siSwati that means "we are not going any further". My grandfather stayed there until he died.

'I was a very small boy at that time, looking after my grandfather's patients. I felt that my grandfather was enslaving me. He would beat me if his cattle did not graze properly. Once the cattle went astray while I was watching. Rather than face another beating, I ran away from the Sikhuunyane homestead. I was ten years old. I ran to a Christian mission. This is where I started schooling. I was the garden boy at the mission house. I washed dishes and worked in the garden. The man of that house was a priest and principal of the mission school. I started going to Sunday school and then to a small primary school. The priest could see that I was learning quickly. But I had some problems. I was becoming very, very ill. The priest at the mission and his family loved me. I was doing so well at my job and in school. They wanted me to get better and felt there was only one way, the modern medical way. The doctors they consulted kept trying all kinds of things to cure me.

'While I was ill I would cry out and they worried that I was becoming quite mad, mentally disturbed, but I was not. Always the sensations and hallucinations would pass, I would feel calm and be normal again. It went on like this until I was 15 years old. I continued with my schooling. Each and every night I would study with this missionary, even though I was having periods of illness. I would do the dishwashing then do my studying. I was at the top of my class.

'But the sickness became worse. The mission people would get down on their knees and pray and pray. They cried, I cried. We felt hopeless. In desperation, they put me on the back of one of their domestic workers and sent me to the hospital. In the hospital I became very, very thin. This is why I am so thin even today. This woman who helped me to the hospital heard that my dreaming or hallucinating continued, though now it was happening mostly during the night. She was advised that I might be possessed. She was told to take me from the hospital to some traditional healers.

'She reported back to the mission, but they were uncertain about this. They agreed, though, to try anything. They cared only for my well-being. The woman took me to the traditional healer's homestead at Komatipoort in South Africa. They started to beat the drums to see if my ancestors would come out to test whether I was possessed. They beat the drums to help me. Hearing the drums, I started screaming. This was the ancestors coming out of me. I stayed at this place and completed my training. It was not an easy thing, it was not something that I was happy with. I was so sick.

'Finally, though, I was with people who understood my condition, could protect me and heal me. I started crying out louder, throwing myself on the ground, tearing off my clothes. The drums beating, I became possessed. Each and every day the drums were beating so my ancestral spirits came nearer and nearer. They gave me herbal medicines to cleanse my body until I recovered. Then I underwent the inyanga training. I was thin but becoming very strong.

'This is how the ancestors got me to training. They were putting me on the path I must follow. When I was small, working with my grandfather, I would dream what patients were coming, what diseases they would have, even the types of medicines we needed to collect. We would follow these dreams and prepare for the patients. Always the dreams were correct. I was a good dreamer.'

I specialise in stress and high blood pressure. These conditions have increased tremendously throughout southern Africa because of how people live. Many office workers have too easy a life. They drive to work in a soft car. To reach their offices they go up in an elevator. When they reach the offices, doors open by themselves. The workers sit on swivel chairs to easily turn around, one phone is ringing, now another, they are taking several calls at once. There is a fax coming in, there are newspapers, you can only look at the headlines. There is no time. You have tea, with sugar, it is brought to you. There are lots of papers on your desk.

'You knock off at night, it is the same thing. You drive right into a garage, you open a door, walk maybe five steps. Go to the kitchen, eat lots of oil, drink Coca Cola. Then you go to sleep; the bed is big, soft, plenty of blankets. We no longer walk. We do not prepare our own natural food. We do not sit on mats anymore. We want soft pillows, we wear shoes. If you are walking barefoot, it massages your feet. All the illnesses and problems you have, they work themselves out. You don't have to go for reflexology, it happens naturally. Take off your shoes, walk barefoot. It is a good thing. Children know this, they always take off their shoes. They throw them off. They cannot wait to take their shoes off after school. It is a natural and healing impulse. On the feet there are corresponding points related to all other parts of the body. Let this healing take place naturally as it was intended.

'I value cooperation with the medical people. The doctors tell me I have wonderful medicine. They want to know about it and they refer patients to me, but I cannot teach the medical doctors about my medicine and have them treat their patients with it. I specialise in some areas, they specialise in other areas. That is how it works, we refer to each other for our own specialities. Cooperation like this works best. I have a long-established reputation. I receive calls from South Africa and all over the world. I have learned many things too while travelling to visit the spirit medium clans near Bhera, Zimbabwe, healers in Tanzania, Indian medicine people in North America, healers in England and Germany and other far countries. These international friends are now asking how can I help them with this and that type of disease. I have friends in many places, many countries. But there was a time, in 1980, when all these relationships just stopped.'

'Did I tell you about the detention? I was detained for eight months. I was one of King Sobhuza's traditional doctors. The king even sent me to countries to treat other kings. When he died, I was to continue with the new king. The Queen Mother now had to take over. I was helping her. Through my traditional medicine we raised King Mswati, took him to England for schooling. He was a boy then. I went there twice to help the child. I went with the Minister of the Interior, the former Governor of Lobamba and some other elders.

'While we were in England, a problem developed back home in Swaziland. The Supreme Council of State wanted extraordinary powers. They overthrew the Queen Mother. They made up stories. They said the Queen Mother wanted to kill the new king, her own son, and she had sent me to England to do so. When I arrived home, the Supreme Council wanted me to support them. I could not, so they put me in jail in Manzini. Healers, patients, church people, many people continued to come and see me right in the jail. My guards said, "What kind of person is this?" The newspapers said, "Look at Maseko. He is not detained. He lives like a free man, He can walk out to the shops." I used to go the shops by myself and then return to detention. People asked, "How can this be? This man was to have killed the king but now he is walking about freely?"

'The Supreme Council then moved me to Sidvokodvo. When the police were sick there, I treated them. I had my pouch and medicines from home. People were suffering, how could I not help? I was still receiving too much attention and support so they moved me further away to Bhunya. There, health and medical people began to visit me and together we prepared a training programme. While I was in detention my work just continued.

'One day I told the station commander of the jail that I wanted to talk with the Prime Minister. He said I could not. I had had a dream. I saw a cyclone was about to come. I needed to warn him. Finally I was allowed the call. In three days' time, the seniors for the Prime Minister, his izinduna, came to see me. I said, "Take all your cattle and remove them, something is coming." The dream was so powerful that I was crying while speaking about it. I was worried for these people. They reported back to the Prime Minister and followed my instructions. The cyclone came, just as it was in the dream. Their cattle were saved.

'The Supreme Council began to fight among themselves. They went to the Prime Minister and said, "We want Maseko here now." They sent a big car and asked me to rush to them. As soon as I reached them I asked, "Why are you detaining me?"

'They claimed they didn't know I was being held. They said, "You were the king's traditional healer, please carry on with your work."

'I said, "What have you done with the Queen Regent?"

'They said, "Go to the Queen."

'She was under house arrest, being guarded by the soldiers. They let me go to her. When I saw the Queen Regent, she said, "Oh, my child!" She was crying and I was crying, there was no talking.

'Afterwards the Supreme Council released me and drove me home to Siteki in a government car. I can tell you, people in Mbabane and Manzini were pushing me to become a politician. There was much support. It was tempting, but I knew that was not my profession. So my good relationship with other healers and medical doctors and the government resumed.

'I have trained many healers over the years. Even now, my focus is on training, but today I focus on primary health care training to upgrade traditional healers' skills. We share information we are learning from each other and from the medical community. Things are opening up more now. There are good relationships and models of cooperation between the traditional and the modern medical health care systems. This will continue to grow stronger and stronger over time.

'When you see traditional healers wearing herbs, necklaces, beads, certain attires, these are following their particular clans. They are honouring and obeying their own ancestors who guide them. We don't differentiate among the spirits or the ancestors. For me, for instance, Jesus is just like my king, King Mswati here in Swaziland. Jesus is the Christians' king. In England there is a Queen Mother. There are people who do not follow her but if she comes in the room, they will show respect. They will bow down, kneel down to her, she is their ancestor. Again, it is people following their clan, their culture. People have a right to their own beliefs. A person can be possessed in any belief, even in the church. They must work for that spirit, become a minister, perhaps a nun; it is very strong. If you try to take them away from this belief, from this place, they may even die. I can respect another belief if it is not conflicting with my own clan. We can co-exist.'

PH Mntshali –
a college man called by the ancestors

P H Mntshali is a regionally recognised healer and a specialist in cancer. At seventy-seven years old, he travels frequently to Botswana, South Africa and other countries in the region to assist those patients who cannot travel to him. During the summer of 1994, PH made his first visit to the USA, where he met with natural healers, medical doctors and scientists. When home in Swaziland, PH is busy with a large practice. Active in his community, he was responsible for organising a large water project during a recent drought. He is now advocating improvements to their rural roads as well as spearheading a community clinic scheme that will bring traditional healers and government medical staff together in one facility. Like his colleagues in this book, PH exudes tremendous energy and total commitment to healing. Those around him are counting their blessings the ancestors chose to place him in their region.

I was a learned chap. I never dreamed I would be a healer, although my Gran – Gogo in siSwati – was a healer, the best. A sangoma or inyanga is able to tell everything just by looking at you. They receive direct communication from the ancestors. They view the yesterdays and the future. My Gran was like that and at the same time a healer of diseases.

'My Gran did not teach me things about healing when she was alive. She would just take me along when gathering herbs and say "take this, take that" or "do this, do that". It was my job as a child to assist, but she did not teach me things about healing. If you grew up around these things in the homestead, you were not interested at all. Healing is something that is performed only by that one particular person, it is not for everyone. As a child you don't know how she managed to get the healing abilities. The healer is a well respected person and I was just happy to do things for Gogo. One day Gogo gives you a piece of bread, one day Gogo buys you something for school. You are interested in those things, but not the healing side. We did not bother with what was done by the elder people. That was not our concern. It was disrespectful for a child to even ask questions of the elders. Sometimes, at night Gogo might tell us stories. That was the only time we children could ask questions of Gogo, like, "Why did the animals and plants talk to us once but now they do not?"Ä' Things like that were on our minds.

'Gogo arranged my primary and secondary schooling. She bade me goodbye from Zululand when I first went to the College of Agriculture in Cape Town, just after the war, in 1945. She said, "Look, hold onto my stick." She didn't shake hands. She said, "You will go, but you will come back." That was the last time I saw her alive. When I earned my diploma from agricultural college, I went to work for a private company in Port Elizabeth. I had advanced my skills and specialised in textile wool sorting for industry.

'I was not completely happy in Port Elizabeth. I did not feel settled there. Finally I left my company for a job as a dairy foreman at a nearby farm. It was a good modern farm with sheep and goats. I was worried by a certain manager who wanted me to speak Afrikaans. I only knew English. But he, the manager, didn't understand and would call me a British peasant because I was speaking English. All my communications went through the big boss, the owner of the dairy, because he liked my work. Oh, this made the manager angry. This discomfort on the job was my ancestors' doing. They were trying to point me to Swaziland where I would finally take up my call to become a traditional healer.

'I eventually left Port Elizabeth. The dairy farmer couldn't believe I was leaving. He wrote me a wonderful reference. I didn't want to go back to Cape Town, even though I knew the Cape was better, there were more jobs. I could not understand why I was feeling the urge to leave South Africa and all its many job opportunities. The impulse to go to Swaziland was so strong I had no choice but to follow it. The job market in Swaziland was bleak. I received much criticism for making this choice. I couldn't defend myself and I could not explain. It was just something I had to do, for better or worse. I wrote to the government of Swaziland and to my amazement, received a job offer. In March 1950, I started working in Swaziland as an extension worker with the Ministry of Agriculture. When I arrived, I was the boss of myself. I had to make my own timetable. I had to teach the adults and the farmers. Luckily I had worked with the Xhosa and the Zulus and managed to approach my work with the Swazis easily.'

While I was posted in Piggs Peak, Swaziland, my hut burned to the ground. My small firstborn child was rescued, but my father died. It was immediately after this that Gogo started coming to me in my dreams. She always came at night. There was a certain donga with many trees nearby. When I went to the trees in my dreams, three species stood out. She told me to go and find these trees. I would get up and walk with her in my dream. We would both dig muti. I decided to actually go to that very tree during the day while I was awake. To my surprise I found the trees and the herbs she discussed, exactly as they were shown to me in the dream. I picked the herbs. I brought them home and put them in my house.

'Gogo came back in my dreams the next night and ordered me out again. She showed me another tree and where to dig. I went out the next day – I had confidence now that the tree would be there just like in the dream. I found the tree and dug and found the roots. But Gogo did not explain what the roots and herbs were for. In the afternoon following one of these night visions, a man in my office came to me complaining of some soreness. I thought of the things I had gathered. I brought them to work the next day and made some tea for him. I said, "I don't know what this is but try it. It may help, I am not sure."

'The man tried it and felt better. He came back and said, "You are a healer."

"No, no," I said, "I am not a healer."

'I did not want to be a healer. A few days later the same man returned, praising me, and asking for more treatments. He brought other people with him, as many as twenty at a time. People began to say that I was a healer, that I could help with some ailments. All this time I was still a full-time agricultural field officer. I was not slightly interested in healing. The very idea of being a healer annoyed me.

'Gogo kept coming to me in my dreams. I began to think I must accept this. Gogo was a healer, perhaps now I have to take this on. I seemed to have no choice. It was very disturbing. It went on like that for years. People started coming from other regions, teachers even came to me. Then, a man came from Zanzibar. He was a black Arab, not a black African like me. He was my neighbour. When he ran short of tea, he would come over to my home and ask for some. This man from Zanzibar saw people come to my place for treatment. He said, "You are a friend to me, I will give you something. You are ready to go and strengthen (protect) the homesteads and the people. Now, you are going to charge goats for this service." I thought, now this is becoming a job. I can't do this. Gogo hasn't shown me this. I wasn't happy about it but I did accept it. He said I would be all right doing this. And it went on like this for 20 years.

'During all these years, my Gogo was my only night friend. The man from Zanzibar made me bones with which to consult and diagnose. Between 1956 and 1957 he made these things for me. These bones began to tell me stories. When he had told me he was going to make something that would tell me things – this person I can cure, this one is going to die – I had said, "How can these things tell me stories?" I doubted, and was proven wrong. Those bones were a great help to me. They look like ancient dominoes or tiny slabs of wood. One is a male patient, one is a person on a bed sick, one is an ancestor of the home, one is an inyanga, one shows me clearance. It tells me that I can cure this patient. Others show where the illness is, in the chest, in the stomach. If one certain one joins another, it means home dispute, arguments over money. Another one means the ancestors are looking after your home-stead but they want something, some food, some honouring. So I will ask the patient, how long ago was it that you honoured your grandparents? If it has been too long, the patient must pay homage, must remember, must honour the ancestors. This is how these bones worked for me.

'Not anyone can be a healer, or can throw bones accurately, unless an ancestor is willing to work with you and help you. I had been practising as a healer since 1954, eighteen years just with this one ancestor, Gogo. In 1972, the other six ancestors came out. They did not come to me in dreams. It happened when I went to a traditional healer training centre here in Swaziland. I was already old, it was 1970-something. I had white hair. I went to this place only because my two children were at the point of dying. I was not seeking training – I was only desperate to save my children.

'The inyanga at the training site said to me, "These children are suffering from your own consequences. You are now changing your mind. You must leave the agricultural work to qualify as a healer. Your other ancestors want to come out now. They are tired of waiting for you. It is only one ancestor that is working with you, for all these many years." I only know my night friend is Gogo. The healer says, "Yes, but there are more, they want to come out. They are only touching the children so that you will wake up. They want to get your attention." My children had always been healthy. They were raised with the ways of inyangas and herbal remedies. I treated them, they were never even in the hospital. You see I was a modern man, I owned a car, I had a big garden, I had engines on my homestead pumping water. I did not want to be a healer and have to give these things up, but I decided my children must not die. I had better take this advice.'

I went to the site. I sat in a hut and was covered with white cloth. We were many, all covered and sitting there. The drums were making wonderful noise, we were very happy. It was joyous. The healers were all serious about it, but happy. On the first day, I was so worked up, I started to lose my senses. I put my head up and looked around, I said, "What sort of thing is this?" They hadn't given me anything to swallow, no oils on me, no herbal drinks, just the constant drumming. I jumped up and threw off the cloth. I thought it was useless. I was cross with the trainer. I could feel that something was happening to my body and with my mind. I did not feel in control. The master healer took me gently by the hands, had me sit again and covered me with cloth. The drums finally stopped and I fell asleep.

'Early the next morning, about 4 am, we woke up and they did the same thing. I could hear myself crying loudly but not in my voice. Somebody came out of me and gave his name. I knew the name. He spoke fast, fluent Zulu. I didn't know what he was saying, he only spoke through me. I could hear myself speaking, but I was not having thoughts. You see it is somebody's voice, not yours, you are just a mouth. You are just an instrument. Mind you, once the ancestors go, you are dog-tired. You cannot remember anything. In such a training, the master healers, the trainers, are responsible to tell you exactly what the ancestors have said. That is their job, to be precise, to remember correctly.'

Khumbulile Mdluli – from schoolgirl to healer

During healer training, Khumbulile met and years later fell in love with her trainer's son. Prior to their wedding she began to feel uneasy about the marriage, but decided to go against this feeling and marry. In time, Khumbulile's growing skill and reputation began to overshadow that of her husband. When her father died, it was the responsibility of a male family member to return to the parents' homestead and support the mother. No one stepped forward. Khumbulile, against tradition, returned home to support her mother, sister and ten children, five of whom were her own. Her husband went to South Africa to seek a new life. Khumbulile sees her husband once a year and does not receive any support for their five children, yet she does not blame him for her hardships. She explained that they had both gone against a greater intuitive feeling and paid the price. A great promoter of formal education, Khumbulile makes sure that her children attend primary and high school. Though the school fees leave her strapped for cash, she seems to manage. Her homestead is a happy one. They all seem to take these challenges in their stride.

Khumbulile participates in and delivers health training for private and public organisations. Her speaking engagements have taken her to countries throughout the southern African region and to the USA. Medical doctors and healers from abroad have found Khumbulile through dreams. Often surprised to find their way to her modest rural home-stead, they have visited and returned, to share healing techniques and to study. Khumbulile received her calling to heal as an adolescent. It was the beginning of her having one foot in the modern western world and one in the traditional world. With her strong values as regards formal education, it was not an easy time to be possessed by the ancestors.

T he ancestors began to call me when I was 12 years old. Today I have been practising for 17 years in Swaziland, here in Ntfojeni. As a child, my family did not consult healers. It began with suffering. I had pain in my stomach; even when I was sleeping at night I would have this pain.

'One night in a dream I saw a big man come at me with a stick. He beat me. I did not feel anything then, or when I awoke. After that the ancestors came out. My family told me that I was speaking a language they didn't understand. The ancestors would come out, speak through me and I would dance. After this happened people began saying I had gone mad. They told me what I had done but I would have no memory of these things.

'These ancestors gave me a new name in my visions. I told my family my new name was Prince Lamoni Dlamini. It turned out that this was one of our forefathers. I was frightened. I didn't understand what was happening. I would go to church and pray and pray and pray. I con-tinued to go to school. I would attend school two weeks per month, then become ill and not be able to go. At school they often took me to the hospital when I would suddenly lose consciousness. The doctors and nurses could do nothing to help me. My condition would just improve on its own and I would feel good for a time. This illness had a mind of its own. It did not respond to medicine from the clinic or the hospital.

'This illness and confusion lasted years. Schooling became a struggle for me but I wanted to finish my Form Five (twelfth grade) at secondary school. On 7 May 1982 I was to sit my exams, but the ancestors came. They took me to the place where I was to be trained to be a healer. The ancestors told me – showed me – in visions where I was to go. I described the exact place to my sister and she took me there. We went and it was just as I said. The trainer, this woman, she was expecting me. I trained near the Mananga border between Swaziland and South Africa.

'We were twelve in training, one man, eleven women. The training was very difficult. We worked so hard. We wore no clothes from the waist up. We didn't wear shoes, even when it was cold in winter. We had to rise early for ploughing but we were not going to eat the food we were growing. We had to have our own food from home. We went to the river early in the morning and bathed there, even if it was very cold. Then we had to take some medicine of the ancestors. After that we would vomit. We would clean our bodies and go back to the training site. Then the ancestors would come out and we would dance and dance and dance. We were clean and pure now, the ancestors could come out easily. Following this, we returned to work. I trained in these conditions for one year.

'During the day the trainer would hide things and the ancestors would help you find them. The trainer might even say, "What is the colour of the bus that runs to Manzini and returns in the evening?" Even though you had never seen such a bus the ancestors could tell you the answer, speak through you. I would say what colour the bus was, I would answer all the questions, but I would not remember. My trainer, the matron, would tell me what I had said afterwards. The ancestors would come out and say, "I want a red gown, a black gown" – they would tell me what to wear. I also threw bones at training. It came very easily. No one taught me, an ancestor would come out and the bones would speak to me. The possessed healers are all like this with bones.'

The ancestors are clever about getting us to training. They know we are frightened so they make us sick. Going to training is the only thing that makes us healthy. At first we stay in training just to feel better. Slowly we become interested in what we are learning. We enjoy the ancestors coming to us. We begin to like what we must do now with our lives.

'It is difficult starting a new practice. You feel relieved to have finished the training but you have no one to discuss your patients with. You miss your trainer and the expertise of your fellow trainees. You feel very alone. It can hurt your confidence. But as soon as these worries start, your ancestors will come to the rescue and tell you exactly what it is you need to do. The ancestors will not call you to such a difficult training, just to leave you on your own. That does not happen. The ancestors are so happy because you are following their direction, you are doing their work. They become a great help to you and your patients. The ancestors guide and protect you. You begin to realise you are not on your own.

'Over the years I have seen changes in traditional healing and treatments. We are seeing different types of illnesses today than when I first started my practice. We might have a patient who is very ill and we use the medicine we know but it does not help. The ancestors will show us where to find a new alternative to use. They will even show us a medical person we must consult with. A person we can trust and who will respect us.

'We are not always paid for our healing. We must treat those who are suffering, must give them medicine, keep them, feed them. It is not correct, as people think, that the healers are making lots of money. It is not always so. We set our fees but not every patient can pay them so we have to adjust. I like to see my patients feel better. I just like to treat patients. This is my love, this is my reward.'

Zakhele Sibandze –
from policeman to healer

was with Moses, a THO staff member, the day I visited Zakhele Sibandze. It was one of those great African days, bright blue sky, hot but comfortable, plenty of smiles and waves from local people walking alongside the road. I felt on top of the world. It had recently rained and the colours were brilliant. The mountainous drive was dramatic. Moses explained that Mr Sibandze had been a policeman when he was called to become a healer. I couldn't quite get the picture in my head. The policemen I had had contact with in Africa were macho guys, not the sensitive, nurturing types I had come to associate with the healers. I was looking forward to meeting him.

Mr Sibandze works full-time for the Swazi traditional *Tinkundla* system as a clerk, an administrative officer for the Ntfojeni Region. He has a great sense of humour and appreciates the irony of his position, which requires all the government nurses to report to him, a traditional healer, before and after their shifts at the medical clinics in his region. He has been practising traditional healing for twenty-two years. He, like most of the master healers, has little or no time to relax. He sees his patients in the evenings and at weekends. His dream is to complete the traditional clinic he is building, quit his job and devote all his time to healing.

is modest office, a two-room concrete block building, had a huge tree in front of it, but all else around the building was flat and bare. It had that austere government look. My first impression on entering his office was that it was a mess. It was long overdue for a coat of paint and there were papers piled helter-skelter on his desk and on the floor. While taking that all in, he greeted me with such warmth, I liked him immediately. Sibandze pointed out where the King had his residence just beyond the hills behind the government office property. He told me that the King has residences in each of the regions of the country though he spends most of his time at the palace near the capital city Mbabane.

Sibandze was not looking forward to an upcoming visit by the King because it coincided with a holiday. He anticipated a general overindulgence in home-brew during the celebration and was gearing up for the many patients who would come to him, sick from the bacteria found especially in the home-brewed whiskey. The brewing process is not always looked after carefully. It is easy for dirt, twigs, unclean hands and such to contaminate the brew. Sibandze chuckled that every year he counselled people, mostly men, about the dangers and side-effects of taking this brew. Of course, he said, it rarely made any difference. His patients would suffer for days afterwards but then had an entire year to forget about the pain. Human nature is Sibandze's field – and, like the other healers, he has great compassion for our human failings.

In 1969 Sibandze had been with the police force for six years. He was well respected and his superiors saw good advancement opportunities for him. Suddenly his life changed, with no warning. He would go to work early in the morning feeling fine but at 11 am an ordeal would start. First, he would feel a strong headache, like a migraine. It was so painful he wanted to scream. Then he would have trouble breathing and have a severe pain in his chest. Each time the police rushed him to the hospital. Each time he reached the hospital, his pain would be gone, his breathing returned to normal. The doctors were puzzled. He was transferred to a hospital in South Africa. He stayed under observation in Johannesburg for six months, the doctors found no cure. Once released from the hospital, he continued to suffer from headaches, chest pains and dizziness.

At the time there was a medical officer in Malkerns, Swaziland, whose wife was a traditional healer. She heard about Officer Sibandze and thought he might be troubled by emalodti (ancestors in siSwati.) She went to him and said, 'The ancestors might be trying to possess you. You may have been chosen to become a healer.' This was unacceptable. He was flabbergasted. As a child, his parents had never consulted traditional healers. This was a foreign and even foolish thing. Sibandze's father was an educated Christian minister. His family went to medical doctors. He knew without a doubt that this healing business was not for him. His physical symptoms failed to improve. His pain increased and he wanted to die. At that point his family began looking after him, never leaving him alone, hoping to prevent a suicide attempt.

At the end of June 1970 he disappeared. This was made more incredible by the fact that his extended family and friends were vigilant about watching his movements in order to protect him. He was not aware and does not remember what happened. Somehow, he travelled right across the border to a place in Mozambique where he had never been before. His story follows.

When I awoke in this place, I noticed I was well. I had no headache, no breathing problems. I was thrilled just to feel healthy. That was all that mattered. I learned I was with Shangaan traditional healers in Mozambique. All were wearing the emasiua, the bangles worn by healers. I had come to be trained as a healer. Before I disappeared, I saw my trainer's homestead in a dream. This inyanga was standing at the gate waiting for me, in the dream. When I awoke and saw her, I remembered her vividly from the dream. I don't remember travelling to this place but it looked exactly as it had in my dream.

'I became interested in the training only because I felt better there. If I had to train to be a healer to feel better, I was willing to do it. I would have done anything to feel better again. During the training, my ancestors would come to me in night visions and take me out to gather medicines. The ancestors were good to me. I learned quickly and enjoyed myself. After two years at my trainer's homestead, I began doing my work there as a healer. I was seeing patients, collecting herbs, treating people and building my experience in traditional healing.

'Meanwhile, back home I was listed as a missing person. The police suspected I was already dead. The Director of CID (Swaziland Criminal Investigative Department), a British man, came down to the training site to see if I was alive or dead. He was surprised but no longer worried. He saw me practising traditional healing. It didn't matter that such an odd thing could happen to me, he was just relieved that I was well and safe. After that, I received donations from the police officers to help me while I was still in training. I had made quite a name for myself in a short police career but still this show of support was unusual. It surprised me that my police co-workers recognised my ability as a healer and sought me out early on my return to Swaziland. Even the Commissioner of Police came as a patient. I was surprised to see a Commissioner of Police coming to see me, kneeling to me. In our custom, a person kneels to pay respect to the King, to a chief or maybe a prominent traditional healer. This practice is reserved for people of great stature. A Police Commissioner paying this kind of respect came as a great shock to me. I was awkward with this special treatment. You know the Commissioner is the boss. I am not a boss, only a healer.

'The Commissioner of Police asked me to return to police work. I said no, I am not going back now because I have to do my healing. This is what I love now. Such a surprise, such a surprise. I only can shake my head.

'I was in my early twenties when I received my calling to become a healer. I have been practising since then, twenty-six years. The only interruption was when my father died. I had a quarrel with my brother when my father died. He said, "You are causing some sort of darkness, causing people at home to die." He thought I was disturbing things. He was a Christian and thought my patients were causing this darkness. In an effort to restore peace, I stopped healing for two years. I stopped treating people. It was hard not to treat people. I missed it terribly and I never felt happy or settled.

'In looking back I realised that I had actually had only one patient who died. He came to me at night, very ill, and died the next morning. His illness was too advanced for me to offer help. In all these years, that is the only patient of mine that has ever died. It became clear that I had to return to healing. Today I am treating some people at my brother's home. He sees my sick patients getting better. Over time he has come to understand my calling. There is no more quarrel between us.'

Nomsa Vilakati – healed by the ancestors

ike many of her colleagues, Nomsa never considered becoming a healer. In fact, if she saw a healer coming her way on the road, she would cross to the other side. She was afraid of traditional healers. Raised in the Zionist faith, she attended church regularly. When she was twenty years old, she began to feel an extreme and inexplicable discomfort when she attended church services. As soon as she left the church she would begin to feel fine again. At the same time Nomsa began having recurrent dreams. In one dream she was walking on the ocean and along the sea shore.

Nomsa recalls the dreams from fifteen years ago as if they happened yesterday. 'On the seashore I would see a big snake, it was like lightning. The snake had several heads and was coming from the sea. After these dreams of the snake, another dream followed immediately. In this dream a large fish swallowed me. I stayed inside the fish for seven days. After this time, the fish vomited me out. I saw and heard an old man beating conga drums, like the drums of the traditional healers. He said, ''Here comes the healer.'' He was saying this about me!

'After these dreams, I would not be able to sleep. I was too shocked, too frightened. In the centre of my head and in the bottom of my spine, I felt as if there was an opening, like a tube. I could feel a bright, bright light and air going through me. I could feel this even when I was awake. I would start looking around, wondering what was in the house. I was searching on the bed, under the mattress, looking for something that must be very dangerous. Then I had one last dream before I went to begin my traditional healer training. In this dream I was on the shore. A man came to me. He straightened up my head and my back, my hands and fingers, my arms and my hair. After that he gave me herbs, in the dream. He was a healer, my ancestor. He was preparing me to become a healer.

'Two nights before going to my training, I heard some voices talking to me – but it was not a dream, I was awake. The voices said, "You are going to be trained as a traditional healer. You must stop using creams on your face and body. You must just bathe and leave your skin and hair as it is." I respected this and stopped these treatments and creams. I thought it could not harm me, I might as well try it. On the night before I went for training, I heard voices again, but they were many now. They came and said, "You are to be trained to be a healer, we want to work with you. There is no time to be wasted, you must now go for training."
'

Following the dreams and the voices, Nomsa left her home in the middle of the night, alone. She left her front door open and began walking in her nightgown. There was no one staying in her house. In recalling the experience she is shocked that she could have done this. Her neighbourhood has a relatively high crime rate. This was an unsafe thing to do considering the high incidence of break-ins and theft. Yet her house was not harmed; nothing in it was touched even though the door remained open. Nomsa has no memory of walking through the capital city, in the middle of the night, in her nightgown, down Malagweni Hill, a curving and notoriously dangerous road with the highest number of car accident deaths in the entire country, down into the Ezulwini Valley, a distance of approximately fifteen miles from her house.

The next morning Nomsa woke and found herself sleeping at Mrs Ntombemhlophe Dube's traditional clinic. She knew she had travelled from Hilltop to the Ezulwini Valley by foot and that she had not been bothered or harmed during the long walk. She had a strong sense that she had never been in danger. It made no sense to her, yet she was sure this was the case. No matter how hard she tried to remember, however, she had no recollection of any details of her journey.

Mrs Dube was not prepared for her. She had just completed a two-year training programme with a group of healers who had found her exactly as Nomsa had. The training had been all-consuming and left her little time for her own family. She was exhausted and looking forward to a well-deserved rest. Mrs Dube was flabbergasted and upset that now, after this sacrifice, the ancestors might have chosen yet another trainee for her. She couldn't believe or accept this. She made Nomsa comfortable but warned her that there was some misunderstanding, some mistake and Nomsa would return to her home and be led to another trainer. However, Mrs Dube was contacted in her dreams by Nomsa's ancestors. These ancestors spoke to her and made it clear that she must accept this assignment. After that dream, Mrs Dube knew as certainly as Nomsa knew, that there was no mistake. Nomsa was to stay with her, training for two years.

'Modern doctors do refer patients to me,' says Nomsa. 'The medical people are helpful. For instance, they can replace liquids in a patient that has been dehydrated. The hospital can also provide a blood transfusion when necessary. There is good cooperation with the medical people. My ancestors help me to know which doctors I should work with. They tell me which patients to refer, what treatment they need and where they should go. It is very clear to me how this cooperation should and does work.'

Nomsa found herself in a medical facility as a patient early in 1993. While repairing her roof, she fell and injured her back. She asked to be taken to the hospital because she wanted an X-ray of the bones. Nomsa tells what happened next. 'The doctors took an X-ray and found two small bones lying slipped, next to one another. I was admitted to the hospital. This all happened on a Thursday. In the hospital, I could barely move. I was paralysed from the neck down. I had to use a bedpan. It was very painful even to move my head. I could not even change position in my hospital bed. The doctors said I should expect at least a three month hospital stay. I would require long treatments and eventually physical therapy.'

This was very bad news as Nomsa is a physically active person. In 1992 she won a regional traditional dancing contest held in South Africa. There were more than 2 000 contestants. She is very self-sufficient. Repairing her roof is just one of many manual chores she does to maintain her house. She has no car and walks many miles on a daily basis. This was a devastating injury for her.

Nomsa continues, 'That Sunday night, I fell asleep and was possessed by my ancestors. I got up out of bed by myself. I walked to the bathroom, used the toilet, returned to my bed and fell asleep. I was talking in the ancestor's voice and some of my roommates in the hospital ward noticed. They were shocked that I could do this. The next morning, I did not remember any of this. The other women and nurses told me about it. Even the doctor who examined me that day was surprised. He told me I could be released the next day. He said he couldn't explain what had happened but my bones were healed and I was ready to go. It was my ancestors. They did not want me in the hospital. They came to return me home.'

Occasionally – inexplicably – in my interviews of the traditional healers, I would 'lose' parts of my interviews. Once, I had taped a lively two-hour discussion with Nomsa. Anxious to write down one particular story, I raced home. When I tried to transcribe the audio tape to my computer, I found a twenty minute blank patch on the tape. I could even hear my voice at regular intervals, testing to be sure the tape player was recording. All was in order. Her voice should have recorded. To make matters worse I couldn't remember the story I had been so interested in. The next time I visited Nomsa I asked her about it. She couldn't remember the story either, but was amused. She said it wasn't important. I was to trust that I had what I needed from the story and was to let the rest go, as she already had. It had vanished because its purpose had been served. If I was truly to write about it, the infomation would come again. I would always get what I needed, nothing more, nothing less.

Nomsa didn't always have this incredible faith that the universe, or the ancestors, would provide. One of my favourite stories is an example of the early doubts with which she struggled. Shortly after Nomsa returned home from two years of training her ancestors told her in a dream to build an additional room to her two-bedroom structure. This room was to be used only for traditional healing business and must be sacred. The idea of building this addition haunted Nomsa. The idea of a single-purpose room bothered her, but more importantly, she didn't have the six hundred Emalangeni (R600) to buy the materials. A new healer building a small practice, she had no resources. It was impossible and she worried that she was not able to do as the ancestors had asked.

In the midst of these worries, Nomsa had another dream. In this dream, the ancestors told her to go to the bus terminal in the middle of downtown Mbabane just before dawn, by herself. She knew she had to do this but it was not safe to walk the five miles in the dark alone. Nomsa braced herself and did as she was told. She made it to the bus terminal with no incident. Oddly enough, the bus terminal was deserted. Usually at this time of day there would be many people preparing to make long bus journeys for work or personal reasons. Nomsa felt frustrated and foolish. She remembers thinking, 'What a fool I am. There is nothing here. What am I going to find that will help me build my clinic? Nothing!' She turned around, determined to return home, when an envelope blew across her feet. She reached down and picked it up. Inside the envelope was exactly six hundred Emalangeni, cash. Nomsa looked around for the person who had dropped it. There was no one. Nomsa took the cash and built the clinic that she still uses today, ten years later.

'The ancestors look after me when I do their work,' says Nomsa. 'I no longer worry in troubled times because I have years of proof that if I follow the guidance of my ancestors, one day at a time, everything will work out as it should. This is not only true for healers like myself, but for all people.

Conclusion

Ancient meets modern

Dr Qhing Qhing Dlamini, Swaziland Ministry of Health, completed her medical training in South Africa then went on to study Public Health at the University of California, Berkeley. Later she specialised in management and administration of public health. She has worked in the medical field for twelve years. Qhing Qhing is highly regarded by both the medical and the traditional community. Compassionate and insightful, she implements policy with a participatory approach that includes the traditional healers. Her accomplishments are nationally acknowledged.

Qhing Qhing explains, 'I have worked cooperatively with healers since 1983. The majority of Swazis, as many as eighty per cent, use traditional healers. Their first point of contact for primary health care is the traditional healer. This is not surprising since there are approximately 8– 10 000 traditional healers, of all types, in Swaziland and only 137 registered medical doctors. In 1983 we were seeing many, many children dying from cases of diarrhoea. This was true in both the traditional and the medical sectors. We decided to have a large campaign to introduce and encourage the use of oral rehydration therapy (ORT) to treat diarrhoea cases. There was resistance from the traditional healers and medical doctors as well. Many doctors were using the drip or administering antibiotics or using other unsuccessful treatments.

'We tend to think the resistance always comes from the traditional side, but there are all kinds of people in both sectors and the resistance to cooperation and upgrading health skills comes from all sides. We have doctors practising in Swaziland who come here, open a practice but never register with the Ministry of Health. This is a common professional practice when coming to a country, to register and show your credentials. We have trouble with these medical people. There is always talk of the healers and witchdoctors doing harm but it also happens on the medical side. We are all human. We have the good and the bad on both sides.

'With the help of some project funding from the United States Agency for International Development, we began to meet with communities to discuss the treatment of diarrhoea and the number of lives that were being lost. It was important not to pass judgement on other treatments being used in the past, only to say: 'Here is something new and we have overwhelming proof that it saves lives. We all want what is best for our patients, try this.' We met with not only traditional healers but all community leaders, including medical doctors and nurses, chiefs, rural health motivators trained in primary health care, prominent religious leaders, political leaders, any and all people who could support and reinforce the use of this ORT. We were desperate to stop the deaths.

'First we did our research to be sure we had a clear and true picture of what was happening around the country regarding diarrhoea cases. Then we decided the correct and appropriate intervention was training. We began training the community members mentioned above. We trained hundreds of people countrywide. This aggressive campaign had such impressive results that we turned to the same method when we were ready to start an early childhood immunisation campaign. Once again there was great improvement as measured by health service indicators. In 1986, the World Health Organisation's 'Health Immunisation Year', following our campaign, the percentage of the population who had been immunised went from thirty-nine to sixty-eight per cent.

'This method of cooperating with the traditional healers and other community leaders is a success. We have gone on to use this participatory community development approach for breastfeeding and the 1987 Aids Prevention campaigns. The 1988 Acute Upper Respiratory Infections campaign started and has decreased the number of patients dying from pneumonia. The healers and others now understand and appreciate the importance of getting a person who is suffering from fast breathing, high temperature and other related symptoms to the nearest clinic, hospital, medical facility.

'In Swaziland, pneumonia kills most patients. The healers were seeing many of their patients die of pneumonia. They were trained and receptive to this available medical prevention and it was another example of when and how the two primary health care sectors, the medical and the traditional, could work together. The healers were happy to welcome a method or intervention that would save their patients. The importance of community development strategies cannot be overemphasised. This method, this way of working with the healers and the communities, is now a standard part of the way we do business. The strategy works and is here to stay.

'At present, we do not have guidelines for medical staff to refer patients to the healers. This is difficult for us without a certification process and overseeing board for the traditional healers. The healers refer patients to the medical side for HIV testing, immunisation programmes, upper respiratory infection intervention, and the like. Our relationship with the healers is evolving and growing. Perhaps over time or generations there may be this standardisation on the healers' side and referrals will be possible. We need a formal body through which to address the healers. Today, THO is that organisation. They work side by side with us to train and communicate with the healers. They are very committed and doing a wonderful job. My best advice to the healers in Swaziland would be to join THO and then to get to know their local doctors and nurses, know what they can offer and take the training that THO and the Ministry of Health offer.

'The two systems of primary health care delivery are different and they should stay that way. For example, when a patient comes to the government hospital it is often in an emergency situation. They have tried the healers or the healers have taken them as far as they can go. Now they want the doctor, the nurses, the modern western technology. The best way is for the patients to use their own discretion and decide for themselves when to go to a traditional healer and when to use the medical side. There is definitely a place for both and I imagine that always will be and should be the case.'

Dr Thandi Magdalene Malepe is a clinical psychologist at the Swaziland Psychiatric Centre in Manzini. She received her training at the University of Vienna, then went on to study addiction behaviour in London. She has had a practice for sixteen years. Dr Malepe is unique in that she also completed and graduated from a traditional healer training programme.

'I am a Swazi but I grew up in South Africa,' Dr Malepe begins. 'I did not have any contact with traditional healers while I was growing up. It was only when I came to work in Swaziland that I got involved with the traditional healers. Swaziland is very involved with traditional healing methods. The King, the royal family, all of them consult with the traditional healers. Whatever they do with the royal traditional rituals and ceremonies, there must always be a traditional healer present. So the nation itself believes very strongly in the traditional healers. Even the very educated and professional Swazis consult traditional healers.

'My patients see traditional healers. Some of our serious psychiatric cases, after some time, get tired of our medication and they stop taking it. They consult a traditional healer. Sometimes they come back in very, very serious condition. They are suffering from malnutrition and so forth. I want to avoid situations like that. The fundamental aim of my meeting with the healers on a regional basis is to promote understanding and increase cooperation. I would like the healers to have a better idea of when they might refer a patient to the hospital, clinic and psychiatric centres. I want to discuss and make clear what our abilities and specialities are so we can work together for the sake of our patients.

'If you are very ignorant about traditional medicine you will not be effective with African patients. I went through and actually graduated from traditional healer training. I wanted to know what they do, how they think, how they treat, how it all works. When you are on the outside you cannot understand or know the whole truth about the traditional ways of healing. You have to get on the inside and learn their language. Now when I have a patient and he says he wants to go see a traditional healer I can say whether it is necessary. I speak the language of the healers, I use their terms and the patients are confident.

'When we first heard about Aids, I thought, "We don't have drug users who inject, yet." Then I remembered the traditional healers and their use of razor blades to make incisions where they apply herbal medicines. I do not advise my patients to stop their traditional treatments and incisions. I just say take your own blade, make sure the blade is sterilised and only used on you, once. Now very many in the rural areas are taking this advice and putting it into action. The Ministry of Health is also cooperating with the traditional healers in getting the word out to all the regions, on Aids, nutrition, hygiene, family planning, sexually transmitted diseases and so on. The government said, "Let's give the healers what they need to know, give them malaria tablets, teach them how to stop diarrhoea, teach the importance of immunising children, the benefits of breastfeeding – all those things. It is important to demystify both the traditional and the medical. Let people have information and understand the types of treatments available to them.

'There are many psychosomatic problems in Africa. For example, I had a patient who had a stroke. He went to a traditional healer who told him somebody had put traditional medicine on his car, on the handle of the door on the driver's side. It was when he touched this that he suffered the stroke, he went lame, suffered stroke-like symptoms. Whenever he touches this handle he suffers a shock, like an electrical shock or charge. I consulted with a traditional healer who has worked with us for years. I said to this healer, ''Our treatment has not worked for this man. Do what you can, we must rid him of this.'' Now after the treatment from this traditional healer he is walking again, he is fine.

'In another case, there was a grown man who thought he was the natural child of the man and woman who raised him. His brothers and sisters believed that too. The mother knew the child's father was in fact another man but chose not to tell him. One day, the real father comes to visit and this man (the son) goes completely lame. They brought the lame man to me. He wanted to slaughter a goat, so we did. I knew what to do traditionally. He had faith in me and in three days he was walking again. I understand what the traditional healers do and can incorporate it into my practice as I see necessary.

'The traditional healer does not so much try to get to the root of the problem as we would in western psychotherapy. The healer is starting with where the patient is, dealing with their illnesses only as far as the patient can take it, at that time. What he does is give the patient faith, some herbal medicine, and says the rules of this medicine are A,B,C. For instance, with alcoholics, they say, ''I am going to give you this powder but you must not touch alcohol. The powder is to be mixed in your tea.'' It could be just some mild herb but it does help him because he believes in the treatment and he does not touch alcohol. It is psychological and it helps him to stop.

'With addiction, I treat the whole family. I go to the family and even speak with the community to explain and help them understand the effects. I explain that the person is affected by the alcohol and that his behaviour changes are signs of the disease working on him. It is not that he is a bad or weak person. In addition, a traditional healer will perform certain rituals with the patient and his whole family. He will impress upon them that they must never put pressure on the patient to take any type of alcohol, not even traditional or ceremonial brew. They must allow that person to participate while having water, juice or something. I have seen this work. It is a dignified way to treat the patient.

'My experience since 1980 is that many addictive people are in fact gifted. They often were ignored in school and at home. We are now trying to create a gifted child programme in Swaziland to identify and help those children. We want to develop their gifts before they are discouraged. They have the genetic makeup, they already have the tendency toward addiction. We want them to develop the gift and not the disease.

'Years ago it was not acceptable for the medical community to work with the traditional healers. Now, we are reaching out to them, we are visiting their clinics. I think a newly graduated traditional healer should have an orientation and welcome from the government, the Ministry of Health. They would receive an overview and feel welcome. Perhaps they would feel more comfortable introducing themselves to their local clinic personnel. The clinic would be familiar with the orientation programme and would be prepared to welcome and work with them. They would be seen as an important resource. We are moving in the right direction. Cooperation between the traditional and medical health care systems will only grow stronger and have great benefit to us all.'

Dr Zama Gama, of Raleigh Fitkin Memorial Hospital, approaches his work and the healers with the patience of someone who understands how long it takes to change attitudes. Born and raised in Swaziland, Dr Gama did his medical training in Nairobi, Kenya. Practising medicine since the 1980s, Dr Gama works in the children's ward of a large hospital in Manzini, the very hospital he was born in.

Dr Gama tells his story, 'My mother was a staunch Christian. My father was an uneducated but very clever man who grew up in the traditional ways and saw problems with it. He decided he wanted nothing to do with things traditional. So I grew up knowing nothing about traditional methods of healing. Only when I came into contact with others at school and at university did I begin to hear about traditional healers. In medical school I learned about the traditional herbs and medicines that are being used. Kenya and other African states have established scientific centres to study traditional medicines and treatments. These are places of science where both sides, the healers and the medical practitioner, can come together and work, can learn from each other. These centres have extracted elements from herbs that are now being used to treat certain illnesses and diseases.

'The herbs have proven healing properties but there are problems related to dosage and impurities. I see these problems in my patients. It is possible for the inexperienced healer to give an overdose of herbal medicines. A herb, if it has an active ingredient, has a limit which the body can take. For adults, that limit may be much higher than it is for children. But for children, an overdose is noticeable and sometimes devastating, like kidney failure. I have seen unusual electrolyte imbalances that I am not seeing in other patients that have the same illness. Gastritis is a good example too. A patient may have taken muti, herbal medicine or treatment, in the wrong dosage and the herb was impure. This causes the electrolyte imbalance.

'When I am called to see a patient, it is because the family has sought help from the healer and the treatment has not been successful for any number of reasons. I may find that the signs and symptoms for that particular disease are exaggerated. The child's condition doesn't look as bad as the child actually is. There must be something else causing this distress. I learn the child has taken muti. Now I understand and can get more information from the parents. I probe to help me understand how I can complement this treatment.

'Most of the rural and even the urban women will pass through a traditional healer before coming here to my offices. We, the medical profession, know that we are the back-up health care delivery system. A Swazi goes to see a traditional healer. If the healer cannot clear up the problem, the patient now consults a doctor or nurse. We must work in a way to acknowledge this orientation amongst our patients.

'I have attended workshops with the Traditional Healers Organisation. In these training workshops, THO members were taught about Aids prevention and how it is transmitted. They discussed early childhood immunisation. In fact, in one workshop I attended they decided among themselves that if a mother brought a child to them (a traditional healer) they would first ask, has this child been immunised? For the healers who have attended this training, it is now standard procedure for them to ask to see the immunisation card. They will ask the mother to take the child to update its immunisations. These are all very good things THO is achieving in its training. I have received referral forms from my patients. Their traditional healers used the form to refer the patient and it gave me some information to work with. The patients were referred at the right time, all was in good order. These referral cards are a very good idea. These two primary health care systems can work well together.

'There is a time and place for both medical and traditional treatments. The traditional healers, for instance, are very successful at treating mental illness. One of the reasons they are, is that they are one with the people. They tend to have higher confidence from their patients. Most of them are very good psychiatrists. They talk to the patient about the things the patient knows. They do this through throwing bones or with other help from the "ancestors". The patient is very comfortable with this. The healer identifies and treats the problem from the patient's point of view. Whereas the doctor or nurse often comes with all the scientific knowÑledge and tries to analyse a problem which is social in nature but with some physical symptoms; we come with an educational base that often clouds the real problem. We come with certain assumptions based on their symptoms.

'The healers are closer to the patients than we are. If a person is sick with a chronic illness, the patient will actually go and stay right at the inyanga's place. You know, I don't think I would take in someone who was ill and have them stay in my house. But that makes that patient a part of the family. This is an especially important contribution with terminally ill patients. It is such a comfort to both the patients and the patient's family that someone still cares and is still trying.

'For now, I think the two primary health care delivery systems, the traditional and the medical, should remain separate, but with much more cooperation. We have the same goal and we must talk. If we have differences, and there are many, the only way we can sort them out is by knowing what the other one is doing. If you believe a healer is interfering with the treatment of your patients, the only way to clear this up is to talk to the healer, because the patient is not going to stop seeing the healer. It is up to the doctor and the healer to understand one another and find a way to work together for the benefit of the patient.

'The generations ahead of us will be much more enlightened and such cooperation will improve. I support good scientific research that helps us understand each other's practice. In the past, healers practised in secret. Now they are much more open and we can learn from each other. All our medications in the medical profession are known, anyone who is trained and has credentials can use them. The information is disseminated and available to all studying medicine. This is how it should be. That is how it will be one day for herbal medicines as well.'

P H Mntshali, Zulu healer, says: 'There are many examples of healers who have developed cooperative relationships with modern doctors. Good traditional healers and doctors both concentrate on the patient. They see what is the best treatment: Is it traditional? Is it medical? Is it a combination of both? They respect both sides. We must bring back a stronger respect and awareness of traditional treatments. We must continue to improve sanitation, hygiene, living standards, especially in the rural areas. Through our professional healer organisations and the government departments of health, we are introducing our traditional healer to these standards. Our children must appreciate that natural medicine is not "primitive". They must have the benefit of both systems, both health treatments. They need to understand both in this new world.'

Khumbulile Mdluli, Swazi healer, says: 'The medical side must come round to working with the healers and the healers must continue referring to the medical side. Today we healers are referring patients for cholera, HIV testing, early childhood vaccination programmes and much, much more. We seek out and incorporate what the medical profession has offered us. Like the oral rehydration treatment, ORT – because of cooperation with the clinics, we now have ORT packets ready to use immediately with our patients. There are many dehydrated, malnourished patients due to the drought. Before, a healer may have been missing an ingredient of the rehydration mix. Now it is ever ready. We also receive condoms from the clinics to distribute to our patients. These are only a few small examples of how we are working together.

'Medical people do not often refer patients to traditional healers because they do not know what the standard is, are not sure how their patients will be treated. The medical side needs more information on the healers. Today there are strong relationships where healers are seeking out a particular doctor and the medical staff is consulting with the local traditional healer. These relationships are strong because the individuals have the patient's well-being at heart. They search for the best treatments and notice which treatments are consistently successful, whether they be herbs or synthetic medicines. But it all takes time, resources and a growing willingness to understand and not judge each others' practice. I have great hopes for health care in the future. Our children and children's children will benefit from the seeds of cooperation started two decades ago.'

Mrs Jekeleza, Swazi healer and sangoma trainer, said: 'When I began my life as a healer, thirty-six years ago, we were scared to visit the Ministry of Health. We were not allowed to visit our patients in the hospital. Today we are invited to accompany our patients to hospitals. Today I can ask a medical doctor to provide a specific service, such as blood work. That doctor will comply and not give additional services but send the patient back to me first with the results. The doctor may discuss the results with me, one health care person to another, but he will not interfere with my patient. You cannot imagine what a huge difference this is compared to when I started my practice.

'We healers are learning how to cooperate with the medical side. From our own experience and from training, we are learning what we can and cannot cure or what diseases are best treated by help from both sides. I am also a trainer of healers so I teach these things in my own training classes. My graduates know when to refer to a doctor or nurse. They know when to refer to another healer who has a speciality they need. We healers have specialities and the medical people have specialities. The job for us all is to know our gifts and our limits. Together these two sides will be stronger than either side standing alone. If we are true healers, we will put our differences aside and continue to devote ourselves to our patients.'

Mrs Dube, traditional healer and sangoma trainer, said: 'The co-operation between the medical profession and the healers is much better than when I first started practicing fourteen years ago. More information is available and we have regular opportunities to get together with other healers to discuss treatments and specialities. When we refer our patients to other traditional healers, we always hear back when the other healer discharges the patient. We cooperate well with each other. Over time, this cooperation will also improve with the medical doctors and nurses. We have developed a referral form because we want to make it easy for the clinics to stay in touch with us.

'We must not give the impression that the modern medical clinics are always clean and maintained to a high standard. This is just not the case. There are some clinics and hospitals I will not refer my patients to because I feel they will actually become more ill or exposed to greater disease at the medical facility. In this way, the doctors, nurses, clinics are much the same as our traditional clinics. To say that all traditional clinics are good and clean can also not be said. It all depends on the people who operate the clinic and the resources available to them to keep up their place. Even a clinic with limited resources can have professional staff, whether it be traditional or modern medical. They can be dedicated to the healing of their patients and keep their patients and their grounds neat, tidy and clean. It comes down to the individuals caring for the patients and the clinics. It is impossible to say that one health care delivery system is better than the other. They are equally important and both necessary.

'Through our healer organisations, we have had a chance to meet and even exchange healing techniques and treatments with traditional healers from other countries. One such visit left me with a deep interest in exchanging more information with American Indian healers who were here. We felt such a strong relationship with them when they visited from America. There is a bond between us. Many of our medicines and treatments, ceremonies and drumming are similar. It was like having brothers and sisters visiting. We cried tears of joy to have spent time with them. There is more we can learn from each other.'

Dr Richard Lemmer, of the South African Trade Mission to Swaziland and Mozambique, did his medical studies in South Africa and began practising medicine in 1983. A general practitioner, Dr Lemmer also has a diploma in occupational health. When we met he was busy working on a master's degree in public health. His contact with the healers began in earnest when he came to live in Swaziland in 1987. As a child Dr Lemmer had no contact with traditional healers. Only after he completed his medical degree did the opportunity present itself. Since that time he has attended traditional healer meetings and training workshops. The healers have a fond place in their hearts for Dr Lemmer and the many doors he has opened for them both in Swaziland and in South Africa.

'In Swaziland, there are approximately 10Ä000 traditional healers. There are not 150 medical doctors in Swaziland. If something is wrong, it is natural for a Swazi to go see the traditional healer who is just down the road rather than try to get into town with no transport to a clinic or doctor many, many kilometres away. We need to understand what services the traditional healer can provide in this first contact with primary health care. We must, on both sides, understand what the gap is.

'I had a patient a while ago who had a growth on his leg. We had a biopsy done and found bone cancer. The only treatment is to have the leg amputated. If amputated immediately it could possibly be cut below the knee. If the patient waits, the cancer will spread up the bone and the entire leg may have to go. It is a very virulent cancer. He was taken to South Africa for the surgery and asked to accept this. He was still a young man and strong. But his family said it was not in their tradition to have a part of your body cut off like this. They took him to a traditional healer. I don't know how he was treated. When I saw him the next time, his entire leg was very swollen. It was very sad, there was nothing we could do for him at this stage. It was then that the family recognised there was nothing further the traditional healer could do for him. He needed to go with the modern medical diagnosis to live but he had waited too long. The cancer had spread so quickly that he would die within two weeks' time.

'Even very well-educated Swazis, professionals themselves, will consult a traditional healer. They use both modern and traditional systems. I think they make a choice based not on the quality of clinical care but more on a level of comfort. Say a person works in an office here in Mbabane. He goes home for a week to a rural homestead and becomes sick. He'll go to the nearest traditional healer that his community uses and respects. That is a comfortable thing to do. He may see a doctor when he returns to Mbabane if the illness or ailment persists. There is also the area I call traditional thinking, where a patient thinks he is being haunted by forefathers, by ancestors. He feels he has done something wrong but he doesn't know what. He knows that to clear his conscience or to clear the community's conscience he must go to the healer and have the healer sort it out with him. This the healers can do.

'There is a traditional belief system that is bound up in healing that the southern African cannot or maybe should not, get away from. Healing is a strong part of the traditional and historical fabric. There are many people who are anti traditional healers but there is no question about it, they have been here much longer than we, modern medicine, have. In general practice many of the patients that come to see the doctor do not need medicine. They need to talk. They might have something physically wrong with them but much of the problem is psychological. This is just one area where the traditional healer plays a very important role.

'In the African tradition a person can believe himself sick. This happens to westerners too, all the time. We are just not as aware of it. Africans believe they have done something wrong. That is why they are sick. The healer may give them a herbal remedy to drink and the patient feels better because they believe they are better. They believe the healer is helping them. The healer has more time with the patient. I cannot overemphasise how important this is. A patient suffering from stress in an urban area comes and spends time at the healer's clinic. The patient is looked after, fed and can rest. Now what is the difference between that and a western health spa? It is the same.

'In South Africa alone, there are 250 groups representing the traditional healers. The government, professional organisations, donors and funders cannot talk to 250 groups. It is too disjointed, too cumbersome. It is not a manageable way to make decisions and have discussions. The government says, "Please send us someone to talk to, we cannot talk to all these groups. Organise yourselves so we can move forward and work together." There has to be one major, umbrella organisation and certification board that can represent this profession to the government, to other countries.

'In Swaziland, we are fortunate to have the Traditional Healers Organisation (THO), the prominent agency representing the healers today. THO is raising the levels of understanding among the healers, raising hygiene and sanitation standards, demonstrating the importance of clean water, vegetable gardens, good nutrition. They are teaching about the spread of Aids, the importance of immunisation programmes for children. They have an ambitious programme.

'Standards of treatment, dosages, hygiene, sanitation and sterilisation at the traditional clinics are needed. There must be some group that guarantees, that oversees, this standard. It is only then that the cooperation between these two systems, traditional and medical, can move forward in an institutional way. Nhlavana Maseko, the president of THO, has often told me that the healers need good clinics. They are in dire need of a clean, reliable running water supply, good roads, and a decent means of communication. Most of these are not health problems, but basic infrastructure problems. THO is trying to raise the infrastructure standard because they know this will impact the health care standard as well.

'Eventually these standards will improve and cooperation between the medical and the traditional will become commonplace. An ongoing type of cooperation and responsiveness is a better and more practical way of working together than integrating the two systems. A good referral system between them would be the best. The first traditional healer I met in South Africa today has an impressive relationship with the local medical clinic. If he sees a patient he knows he cannot treat, he calls the nurse. He tells her what the patient's symptoms are and asks them to come fetch him and they do it! The clinic comes and collects the patients. It is a beautiful example of cooperation, of a good working relationship between the two. They are supportive of each other. They talk and share information. It is the best of both worlds.

'There is and always will be an important place for the healers. People who are working against the healers, trying to displace them or close down their health care delivery system, are simply fighting a losing battle. My preference is to create a formal cooperative relationship, remembering that with all health professionals, the patient's health is the most important thing. These healers you are writing about are really the living example of how such cooperation between the two worlds can work. They are the role models.'

Glossary

amaDlozi 'Ancestors' in Zulu.

Bandzawi In siSwati, an ancient type of ancestor whose language is no longer spoken. When 'possessed' or in trance, traditional healers may speak the language of the Bandzawi.

Donga Ditch.

Emalangeni Currency of Swaziland.

Emalodti 'Ancestors' in siSwati.

Gogo Grandmother.

Induna (pl. izinduna) Headman, councillor.

Inyanga Herbalist; traditional healer.

Lobolo The bride price which, in Swazi custom, the husband's family must pay to his intended's family. This will be cattle, money and gifts.

Muti Medicines used for treatment by the traditional healers.

Rondavel A traditional small round hut, often one room.

Sangoma Traditional healer; possessed healer.

siSwati The national language of Swaziland and the Swazi people.

Tinkundla system Swaziland's traditional system of administration.

Index

Herbs and other natural health products and information are often available at natural food stores or metaphysical bookstores. If you cannot find what you need locally, you can contact one of the following sources of supply.

Sources of Supply:

The following companies have an extensive selection of useful products and a long track-record of fulfillment. They have natural body care, aromatherapy, flower essences, crystals and tumbled stones, homeopathy, herbal products, vitamins and supplements, videos, books, audio tapes, candles, incense and bulk herbs, teas, massage tools and products and numerous alternative health items across a wide range of categories.

WHOLESALE:

Wholesale suppliers sell to stores and practitioners, not to individual consumers buying for their own personal use. Individual consumers should contact the RETAIL supplier listed below. Wholesale accounts should contact with business name, resale number or practitioner license in order to obtain a wholesale catalog and set up an account.

Lotus Light Enterprises, Inc.

P O Box 1008 CTH
Silver Lake, WI 53170 USA
262 889 8501 (phone)
262 889 8591 (fax)
800 548 3824 (toll free order line)

RETAIL:

Retail suppliers provide products by mail order direct to consumers for their personal use. Stores or practitioners should contact the wholesale supplier listed above.

Internatural

33719 116th Street CTH
Twin Lakes, WI 53181 USA
800 643 4221 (toll free order line)
262 889 8581 office phone
WEB SITE: www.internatural.com

Web site includes an extensive annotated catalog of more than 10,000 products that can be ordered "on line" for your convenience 24 hours a day, 7 days a week.

PLANETARY
HERBOLOGY

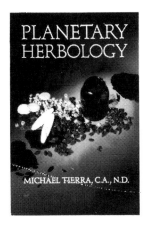

Michael Tierra, C.A., N.D.

$17.95; 485 pp.;
5½ × 8½ paper; charts.
ISBN: 0941-524272

Lotus Press is pleased to announce a new practical handbook and reference guide to the healing herbs, a landmark publication in this field. For unprecedented usefulness in practical applications, the author provides a comprehensive listing of the more than 400 medicinal herbs available in the west. They are classified according to their chemical constituents, properties and actions, indicated uses and suggested dosages. Students of eastern medical theory will find the western herbs cross-referenced to the Chinese and Ayurvedic (Indic) systems of herbal therapies. This is a useful handbook for practitioners as well as readers with a general interest in herbology.

Michael Tierra, C.A., N.D., whose very popular earlier book, *THE WAY OF HERBS,* led the way to this new major work. He is one of this country's most respected herbalists, a practitioner and teacher who has taught and lectured widely. His eclectic background studies in American Indian herbalism, the herbal system of Dr. John Christopher, and traditional oriental systems of India and China, contributes a special richness to his writing.

To order your copy, send $19.95 (postpaid) to:
Lotus Press
P.O. Box 325
Twin Lakes, WI 53181
Request our complete book & sidelines catalog.
Wholesale inquiries welcome.